AF699630

Inflation and the Money Supply in the United States, 1956-1977

Inflation and the Money Supply in the United States, 1956-1977

Peter I. Berman
The Conference Board

Lexington Books
D.C. Heath and Company
Lexington, Massachusetts
Toronto

Library of Congress Cataloging in Publication Data

Berman, Peter I.
Inflation and the money supply in the United States, 1956-1977.

Includes index.
1. Inflation (Finance)–United States–Mathematical models. 2. Money supply–United States–Mathematical models. I. Title.
HG538.B388 332.4'1 78-4344
ISBN 0-669-02346-9

Copyright © 1978 by D.C. Heath and Company.

All rights reserved. No part of this publication may be reproduced or transmitted in any form or by any means, electronic or mechanical, including photocopy, recording, or any information storage or retrieval system, without permission in writing from the publisher.

Published simultaneously in Canada.

Printed in the United States of America.

International Standard Book Number: 0-669-02346-9

Library of Congress Catalog Card Number: 78-4344

HG
538
.B388

To My Children

Avram, Gabriella,
Alice, Elena, and Keith

Contents

	List of Figures and Tables	ix
	Foreword	xi
	Acknowledgments	xiii
Chapter 1	**Introduction and Summary**	1
	1.1 Introduction	1
	1.2 Modeling the Monetarist Inflation Thesis	4
	1.3 Findings	5
	1.4 Implications	8
	1.5 Accounting for Unexplained Inflation: 1973-1975	9
	1.6 Policy Recommendation	12
Chapter 2	**A Procedure for Testing the Monetarist Inflation Thesis**	17
	2.1 Introduction and Overview	17
	2.2 Specifying the Monetarist Inflation Model	20
	2.3 Estimating Distributed Lag Models	27
	2.4 Causality Direction	33
	2.5 Predominance of Monetary Inflation	34
Chapter 3	**Testing the Monetarist Inflation Model with an M_1 Specification**	39
	3.1 Introduction and Summary	39
	3.2 Approximating the Correct Lag Specification	41
	3.3 Sensitivity Analysis of the 10-Quarter-Lag M_1 Model, 1963-1971	42
	3.4 A Closer Look at the 10-Quarter-Lag-M_1 Model	46

3.5 A Post-1971 Stability Testing of the 10-Quarter-Lag M_1 Model 50
3.6 Testing for Pre-1963 Structural Change 54
3.7 Testing Causality Direction 59

Chapter 4 **Specification Analysis of Money Aggregates Other Than M_1** 77

4.1 Introduction and Summary 77
4.2 The M_2 Specification 79
4.3 The M_3 Specification 85
4.4 The Reserve Aggregate Specifications 88
4.5 Niehans's Specification 91

Chapter 5 **A Forward Simulation with the M_1 Model: 1971/3-1975** 93

5.1 Introduction and Summary 93
5.2 An Overview of the Simulation 97
5.3 Does the Monetary Influence Predominate? 99
5.4 A Closer Look at the Forecast Errors 100
5.5 A Suggested Explanation of the 1973/4-1974 Inflation Surge 108

Chapter 6 **The M_1 Model's Inflation Implications for Monetary Policy** 113

6.1 Introduction and Summary 113
6.2 Inflation Associated with M_1 Growth Trends 115
6.3 Post-1978 Inflation Forecasts 117
6.4 An Anti-Inflation Money Growth Policy 118
6.5 Variability of M_1 Growth and Stability of Inflation 121

Bibliography 129

Index 133

About the Author 139

List of Figures and Tables

Tables

3-1	Overlapping and Lengthening Sample Sensitivity Tests, 10-Quarter-Lag M_1 Model, 1963-1971	43
3-2	Straddle Sensitivity Tests of the 2½-Year Lag M_1 Model, Quarterly and Semiannual Data, 1963-1971	45
3-3	Lengthening and Overlapping Sample Sensitivity Tests, 10-Quarter-Lag M_1 Model, 1963-1976	52
3-4	Inflation Forecasts with the M_1 Model, 1976-1977	53
3-5	Structural Change Tests, 10-Quarter-Lag M_1 Model, 1956-1971	56
3-6	Comparative 10-Quarter-Lag M_1 Model Estimations, 1956-1976	58
3-7	Sims Causality Test Summary Results for M_1	62
3A-1	Overlapping Sample Sensitivity Tests, 20-Quarter-Lag M_1 Model, 1956-1971	68
3A-2	Overlapping Sample Sensitivity Tests, 10-Quarter-Lag M_1 Model, 1956-1971	69
3A-3	Sideways Straddle Sensitivity Tests, 10-Quarter-Lag M_1 Model, 1963-1971	69
3A-4	Straddle Sensitivity Tests, 5 Semiannual Lag M_1 Model, 1963-1971	70
3A-5	Complete Shiller and Almon Estimations, 10-Quarter-Lag M_1 Model, 1963-1971	71
3A-6	Almon Estimation Residuals, 10-Quarter-Lag M_1 Model, 1963-1971	72
3A-7	Backward Lengthening Sample Sensitivity Tests, 10-Quarter-Lag M_1 Model, 1956-1971	73
3A-8	Sims Tests, 1963-1971	74
3A-9	Sims Tests, 1963-1976	75
3A-10	Sims Tests, 1956-1971 and 1956-1976	76

4-1	M_2 Monetarist Inflation Model Estimations, Variable Lags, 1963-1971	80
4-2	Sims Causality Test Summary Results for M_2	82
4-3	Commercial Bank Time/Savings Deposit (M_2-M_1) Monetarist Inflation Model Estimations, Variable Lags, 1963-1971	83
4-4	Sims Causality Test Summary Results for M_2-M_1	84
4-5	M_3 Monetarist Inflation Model Estimations, Variable Lags, 1963-1971	86
4-6	Thrift Deposit (M_3-M_2) Monetarist Inflation Model Estimations, Variable Lags, 1963-1971	87
4-7	Reserve Aggregate Monetarist Model Estimations, 10- and 15-Quarter Lags, 1963-1971	89
4-8	Sims Causality Test Summary Results for Total Reserves	90
5-1	Forecast Inflation, Actual Inflation, and Forecasting Errors, 1971/3-1975/4	97
5-2	Actual and Predicted Cumulative Price Indices, 1971/3-1976/4	101
5-3	Comparative Controls Simulations, 1971/3-1972/4	103
6-1	Post-1978 Inflation Forecasts with the M_1 Model	118
6-2	Inflation Forecasts under Annual M_1 Growth Reduction Proposals	120
6-3	Cycles in M_1 Growth about Selected Trend Rates	123

Figures

6-1	Simulated Inflation from Cycles in M_1 Growth about a 4 Percent Trend	124
6-2	Simulated Inflation from Cycles in M_1 Growth about a 5 Percent Trend	125
6-3	Simulated Inflation from Cycles in M_1 Growth about a 6 Percent Trend	126

Foreword

The research for this study of inflation and the money supply was carried out by Dr. Peter I. Berman in his capacity as senior economist at The Conference Board. As such, it represents part of the Board's continuing research program in the area of economic policy. In this work he was assisted by associate economists Steven Malin and Linette Stein. However, Dr. Berman's far-reaching policy conclusions and recommendations represent his personal views. The Conference Board takes no position on public policy matters.

Some of the results of the empirical research were used in *International Influences on U.S. Inflation, 1971-1976*, a separate, unpublished study prepared by Dr. Michael E. Levy, director of the Board's Economic Policy Research Department, under a contract with the Office of Economic Research of the U.S. Department of Commerce.

Kenneth A. Randall
President
The Conference Board

Acknowledgments

I wish to extend my very sincere appreciation to Professors Thomas Mayer, Phillip Cagan, Jagdish Handa, Dean Dutton, Jürg Niehans, William Poole, Chaman Jain, Robert J. Gordon, Jonas Prager, and Sharon Gadberry for their valuable critical comments and suggestions on an earlier draft.

At the Conference Board, many rewarding hours were spent in discussion with Michael Levy. I benefited from extended discussions with Elliot Grossman and Steven Malin, both of whom read through the entire manuscript. Helpful comments were also received from Edgar Fiedler, Daniel Creamer, and Lewis Bergman. Statistical assistance was provided by Linette Stein and Steven Malin. Many thanks are due Sylvia Liebman for typing assistance. And I wish to thank both Michael E. Levy, director of the Economic Policy Research Department and Edgar Fiedler, vice president for economic research, for their support and encouragement.

None of those mentioned above are responsible for any errors which may appear in this study. Also, the views expressed herein do not represent the position of The Conference Board.

Acknowledgments

Inflation and the Money Supply in the United States, 1956-1977

1 Introduction and Summary

1.1 Introduction

The unprecedented peacetime inflation throughout the industrialized economies in the 1970s and its continued persistence despite the severe 1974-1975 recession have encouraged a vigorous interest in the origins of inflation.[1] In the United States inflation has averaged about 6 percent, more than double the figure for the 1950s. And between late 1973 and late 1974 inflation accelerated from 7 to 12 percent and then decelerated even more abruptly early in 1975. One of the many explanations for the continuing increase in the price level is the growth in the money supply, a claim often expressed in Milton Friedman's familiar phrase, "Inflation is always and everywhere a monetary phenomenon."[2] The purpose of this study is to empirically examine whether the money supply has been a continuing source of inflation in the United States over the past two decades.

Explaining inflation in terms of money growth sharply contrasts with the conventional wage/price approach used in virtually all econometric models of the United States economy.[3] The wage/price models satisfactorily explained inflation prior to the 1970s without *any* reference to money growth, but have not been altogether successful in the 1970s. Often called markup models, they explain inflation primarily in terms of the current dollar increase in labor costs over the labor trend productivity gain, roughly 2 percent per annum. Of secondary importance are variables capturing demand pressures in the product and labor markets. The usual finding is that the wage/price elasticity is unity; i.e. current dollar labor cost increases in excess of labor productivity gain are proportional to increases in the price level.[4] Business conditions analysts often note that adding the growth of labor costs to labor productivity gain ordinarily gives a close approximation to the current inflation figure.

Proponents of the conventional approach view with considerable skepticism the controversial claim that the source of inflation, i.e. growth in the price level, is the growth of the money supply. The major issues are the causality or, what amounts to the same thing, the exogeneity of the money supply process with respect to inflation; the stability and precise nature of the money growth-inflation relationship; and the extent to which this relationship has any relevance for explaining the unusual course of the price level in the 1970s. The principal focus of this study is directed at these issues. Before we sketch them, it is worth noting that at the very least there is an association between inflation and money growth. Comparing decade averages of the annual growth of the M_1 money supply (demand deposits at banks and public holdings of currency) and inflation (using the implicit GNP price deflator), we find 2.6 percent against 2.6 percent during the 1950s, 3.8 percent against 2.7 percent during the 1960s, and 5.8 percent against 6.2 percent during the 1970s to date.

In a real sense, the heart of the matter is the causality issue. It is always a bold stand to claim a direct cause-and-effect relationship between a pair of important macroeconomic variables. While in principle nothing precludes such relationships, they seldom receive solid support. If the Federal Reserve both is attempting to influence inflation and at the same time is influenced by current inflation, then money growth is not exogenous with respect to inflation. Alternatively, there is no clear-cut causality direction. To obtain some evidence about exogeneity, econometric causality tests on money growth and inflation are required. To date, these have not appeared in the literature. A major focus of our study is to conduct such tests with a variety of money definitions. To be sure, they cannot prove causality, but they can show whether unidirectional causality is possible. These tests do not resolve the issue, but they do constitute important evidence.

Independent of the causality issue, the money growth-inflation relationship does not have clear implications for the proper conduct of monetary policy unless the relationship can be precisely detailed and its stability assessed. Obviously it matters greatly whether the gradual influence of past changes in money growth upon current inflation extend over one year or five years. It is also important to determine the stability of the relationship. In particular, it is important to know whether the relationship that existed prior to the 1970s continued to be a major determinant of inflation in the 1970s. If not, then the policy implications are apt to be fairly modest. After all, there is a long list of suggested explanations by knowledgeable observers for the peculiar events of the 1970s. Some of the more common ones include the OPEC-inspired quadruple oil price hike; sharp increases in primary commodity prices; militant wage demands; agricultural production shortfalls; synchronized expansion in economic activity among the industrialized economies; dollar devaluation; and adoption of floating exchange rates.[5] A major focus of our study is to carefully examine the pre-1970 econometric money growth-inflation relationships with a variety of money definitions and then forward-simulate the more reliable ones through the 1970s. This procedure squarely faces the issue of whether money growth has any important implications for current monetary policy.

The money growth-inflation relationship is often associated with *monetarism* and is sometimes called the monetarist inflation thesis, although it is by no means the crux of monetarism.[6] The term *monetarism* was first coined by Brunner only a decade ago. For its common denominator, it denotes that changes in the money supply are determined by the monetary authority and are major, *causal* determinants of changes in aggregate demand which are allocated between real output and prices.[7] The broad-based montarist empirical and theoretical challenge to the "new economics" is a major issue in macroeconomics.[8] In a much noticed recent survey, Thomas Mayer presents no less than 12 distinguishing propositions associated with monetarism.[9] Historically, monetarism is linked to the renewed postwar interest in the effects of money on economic activity stemming from Friedman's reformulation of the quantity theory as a theory of the stable demand for money, the Friedman and Schwartz *Monetary History,* the Chicago school, and the work of Brunner and Meltzer.[10]

The monetarist inflation thesis is also associated with the quantity theory of price determination.[11] Originally proposed by Hume in the mid-eighteenth century, the quantity theory suggests that over long periods changes in the money supply and the price level tend to move proportionally with each other. While many economists accept the quantity theory as a rough approximation, a recent far-ranging study by Schwartz suggests that the relationship is best expressed as a proportional one between the price level and the ratio of the money stock divided by national output.[12] Indeed, in a recent survey, Frisch cites the Schwartz formulation as *the* monetarist inflation thesis and is careful to note that the causality direction remains very much an open question.[13]

Whether the quantity theory of prices applies to the near term of several years is also an open question, both theoretically and empirically.[14] Many, if not most, economists maintain that over long periods the quantity of money should not affect real output; the full effects should be realized upon the price level. And it is difficult to find persistent inflations that are not accompanied by persistent increases in the money supply. An unusual position is taken by Andersen and Karnosky of the St. Louis Federal Reserve outpost of monetarism.[15] They claim that the quantity theory holds in the short run of several years and is an integral part of monetarism. However, their econometric evidence, suggesting a gradual adjustment of inflation to the past five years of money growth, is not supported by a rigorous sensitivity analysis nor were causality tests made. In the course of our study we will rigorously test the Anderson-Karnosky formulation.

The money growth-inflation relationship is thus associated with many legions: monetarism, St. Louis Federal Reserve monetarism, the quantity theory in both long and short time frames, a broad-based challenge to the new economics, and Milton Friedman! For the purposes of this study, we define the monetarist inflation thesis as consisting of two propositions:

1. There is an econometrically stable, causal, and powerful relationship between inflation and the growth of the money supply.

2. Money growth remained the continuing and predominant source of inflation throughout the 1970s.

The second proposition squarely faces the issue of whether the thesis is relevant to the 1970s. By inference, unusual nonmonetary effects such as an oil price hike may affect the general price level, but only as a one-time affair. If the thesis is correct, then such unusual nonmonetary effects cannot be a continuing source of inflation. From this perspective, the long list of suggested explanations for the unusual course of the price level in the United States during the 1970s is largely beside the point. Money growth should give about as satisfactory (but not necessarily complete) an explanation of inflation in the 1970s as in the previous decade.

The above definition of the money growth-inflation relationship is considerably less strong than the St. Louis formulation. No mention is made of whether the quantity theory holds in the near term of several years. Indeed, the first proposition is very much in the spirit of monetarism. The problems come with the second proposition; it is a strong statement. Yet for purposes of an empirical test of the thesis, it is worthwhile to regard the tumultuous 1970s as a challenge. Conceptually, first we need to determine whether the thesis holds for the 1950s and 1960s. If there is a solid basis for the relationship in that earlier period, *then* it is sensible to forward-simulate into the 1970s and see what happens. If the simulation results are not clear-cut, the policy implications may be ambiguous. But if the results strongly support the thesis, then we are in a good position to make a policy recommendation. After all, inflation is a very major concern, and any suggested theory should be subjected to strong testing. The 1970s are, in many respects, ideal for that purpose.

1.2 Modeling the Monetarist Inflation Thesis

Ideally, the monetarist inflation thesis should be tested within a fully "fleshed out" monetarist model in which the full effects from the monetary impulse, i.e. change in the money supply, upon both the price level and real output are described. In the monetarist framework, changes in the monetary impulse induce changes in aggregate demand, which are then jointly and simultaneously allocated between changes in real output and in the price level. Considerable discussion has centered on the difficulties of detailing the transmission mechanism whereby the monetary impulse ultimately affects output and the price level.[16] As a practical consequence, the thesis either is tested with an incomplete model or is not tested at all.[17]

Empirically, the advantages of working with a highly aggregated, single-equation, reduced-form type (albeit incomplete) of model to test the thesis are overwhelming. Econometric causality tests are made with pairs of variables, and the single-equation model is the appropriate format. The "natural" way of incorporating the gradual adjustment of past money growth upon the current period's inflation is to use a distributed lag. Unfortunately, correctly estimating these relationships is both challenging and burdensome. And since we want to examine a broad range of money definitions in addition to M_1, a single-equation format keeps the computational burden within bounds. Also, it is well suited for forward-simulation purposes; a major focus of the study is to determine whether pre-1970 relationships hold when simulated into the 1970s.

Conceptually, however, the single-equation approach has limitations and is ill suited for testing the neutrality of money in the near term. We cannot simply bury our heads and focus only on the gradual adjustment of inflation to past money growth. Changes in real output can also induce changes in the price level. Such changes can obviously be induced by aggregate demand/supply effects that are not associated with the monetary impulse. And, inasmuch as the monetary impulse affects real output, there may be effects on the price level through that route. Changes in velocity may also be important. However, if our main interest is the stability of the money growth-inflation relationship, then the real concern is making some provision for the *net* influence of changes in real output and velocity upon the price level. If the net influence of these factors is both variable and important, then they need a specific accounting. But if they can be proxied by a fairly stable trend variable, then a simple accounting may be suitable for our major purpose, which is to determine the *stability* and *power* of the money growth-inflation relationship.

The rewards of this rather simple approach are in the eating. Surely if it proves inconclusive, not much, if any, damage is done to the thesis. However, it is not going to tell us if the quantity theory holds in the short run; the joint interactions on output and price level are not made explicit. The "monetarist inflation model" in this study is a quasi-reduced-form shifting distributed lag of money growth on inflation. A shifting constant term is used to capture the combined trend effects of changes in output and velocity upon the price level. While these effects are no doubt important in the short run, the issue is whether they are highly variable when lumped together; if not, then this accounting may suffice. The penalty extracted from this type of modeling is that while strong results may have clear implications, ambiguous results may simply not be meaningful.

1.3 Findings

a. M_1 Specification

A correctly specified M_1 monetarist inflation model provides unexpectedly strong econometric support for the monetarist inflation thesis. (See Chapter 3.)

Sims test of Granger causality strongly supports the hypothesized unidirectional causality running from changes in M_1 growth to changes in inflation.[18] The correct specification for the M_1 model is a stable 10-quarter distributed lag with uniformly sized weights. Since 1956, this model explains about 70 percent of the variability in inflation. For the 1963-1971 period, R^2 increases to 80 percent and the normally distributed residuals imply that, stochastically, money growth completely explains inflation, i.e. the real sector price effects are adequately captured in the trend term. As expected, the distributed lag shifts over time. In the early 1960s, the constant declined by about 2.5 percentage points.

The 11 weights or individual distributed lag coefficients (one each for the current and 10 previous quarters) by which past values of money growth determine inflation are interesting in several respects. They are identical to one another and are stable over more than two decades; their sum, 1.4 (11×0.13), provides a *biased* estimate of the M_1-price elasticity. Ordinarily, a permanently maintained 1 percent increase in M_1 growth will eventually increase inflation by 1.4 percentage points provided there is no change in the *net* influence of the real sector on the price level. By inference, the quantity theory may not hold in the near term. Also, the Andersen-Karnosky claim that the money-price elasticity is 1 in a money-price model is firmly rejected.[19]

Econometrically, the 10-quarter uniformly weighted lag M_1 model is a powerful model with well-established unidirectional causality, a stable distributed lag, and a high degree of explanatory power. M_1's largest component, demand deposits, is also correctly specified with a 10-quarter lag and statistically is identical to the M_1 model. The remaining component, public currency holdings, is correctly specified with a 9-quarter lag and an elasticity of about 2. The M_1 model is supported by a full battery of sensitivity tests: lengthening sample (forward and backward), overlapping sample, straddle, sideways straddle, and disaggregation. (See Section 3.3.) Almon and Shiller methods give identical estimates, and the major features were confirmed with ordinary least squares (OLS). (See Section 3.4.)

An out-of-sample forward simulation beginning in mid-1971 gives impressive forecasts. For 1976 and 1977, the average forecast error is only about 0.5 percentage point, and the forecast errors do not show any sign of progressive deterioration. (See Section 3.5.) Only one quarter, 1977/2, has a forecast error exceeding two standard errors, 1.6 percentage points. At the very least, the M_1 model is a useful forecasting tool.

b. The Predominance of Monetary Inflation: 1971-1975

To test the second part of the thesis, the 10-quarter uniformly distributed lag M_1 model was forward-simulated, using only out-of-sample money growth data, over the period from mid-1971 to 1975, beginning with wage/price controls and ending two years after the quadruple oil price hike. (See Chapter 5.) In each of the 18 simulation quarters, forecast (monetary) inflation was absolutely larger than the forecast errors, representing real sector price effects not directly captured by the trend term. For the period as a whole, inflation was underforecast by about 2 percentage points [mean absolute error (*MAE*)], and as previously noted, when the simulation is further extended, the forecasts for 1976-1977 are satisfactory. The net effect of the real sector on the price level (other than the effects captured by the trend term) in the simulation period was to permanently raise the general price level by about 4 percent. For the entire simulation period, the price level rose by 33 percent, leaving no doubt that the predominant source of inflation was money growth.

c. M_2 and M_3 Specifications

Monetarist inflation models with M_2 and M_3 definitions of money are unsatisfactory primarily because distributed lags with their major components, time/savings deposits, that is, M_2-M_1 and M_3-M_2, respectively, cannot be correctly specified (see Sections 4.2 and 4.3).[20] Although the estimates are not reliable, the money-price elasticities for M_2 and M_3 are each -0.7, or one-half the size and opposite in sign from that for M_1. A Sims/Granger test with M_2's major component, M_2-M_1, rejects the hypothesized unidirectional causality. Interestingly, a Sims/Granger test with M_2 does give mild support, but that is a spurious result reflecting strong causality for M_1. Similar Sims/Granger test results could be expected with M_3 and M_3-M_2. Sensitivity analysis readily reveals that forward simulations with M_2 and M_3 models (and their M_2-M_1 and M_3-M_2 components) give poor results. If the lag is extended to 20 quarters, a fairly high R^2 can be obtained for a M_2 model, but the lag cannot be correctly specified. The test results leave little doubt about M_2 and M_3 specifications (and, by inference, M_4 and M_5) do not support the monetarist inflation thesis.

d. Reserve Aggregate Specifications

An incomplete sensitivity analysis for the 1960s suggests that both total reserves and nonborrowed reserves can be specified with about a 15-quarter uniformly distributed lag (see Section 4.4). Their money-price elasticities are about 1, and the out-of-sample dynamic forward simulations for the post-1971 period with these models are similar to, but less accurate than, those for a correctly specified M_1 model. Sims/Granger tests with the total reserve specification support the hypothesized unidirectional causality. These *preliminary* findings certainly warrant further study and imply that when properly specified, reserve aggregate models may also provide significant support for the thesis.

The reserve base aggregate could not be correctly specified and was unsuitable for identifiable reasons. (See Section 4.4.) Its currency component has a money-price elasticity of about 2 and was correctly specified at 9 quarters, but the reserves component has an elasticity of 1 and is specified at about 15 quarters.

A brief examination of Niehans's recent suggestion of using the Federal Reserve's government security portfolio as a money proxy also gave unsatisfactory results (see Section 4.5).[21]

1.4 Implications

The implications of the unexpectedly strong econometric support for the monetarist inflation thesis are as follows. (See Chapter 6.) A suggested monetarist interpretation of the late 1973-1974 inflation surge is presented separately in Section 1.5.

(1) The actual course of inflation over the last two decades has been mostly determined by policy actions of the Federal Reserve System. To be sure, the Federal Reserve has had other policy concerns besides price stability, but to the extent that M_1 growth reflects the end product of the Federal Reserve's multifaceted policymaking, there is no mystery about the primary source of inflation in the United States—M_1 growth. The net effect of unusual nonmonetary price effects in the 1970s has been to permanently raise the general price level by 4 percent, well below one year's average increase caused by M_1 growth alone.

(2) For complete price stability (no change in the implicit GNP price deflator), trend M_1 growth of 2 percent is required. (See Section 6.2.) Tying M_1 growth to the average postwar real GNP gain of about 4 percent implies 3 percent inflation. By posting M_1 growth targets the Federal Reserve, in effect, publicly announces its inflation policy. The current M_1 growth targets of 4.0 to 6.5 percent imply 3.5 to 6.5 percent inflation. Continuing 1977's M_1 growth rate of 7 percent implies 7 percent inflation. (Interestingly, conventional wage/price modeling of inflation suggests that wage gains be held to average labor trend productivity gain, about 2 percent, for price stability. Perhaps 2 percent is a major number.)

(3) The inflation prospects are gloomy. (See the forecasts in Table 6-1.) Another year of 7 percent M_1 growth will raise inflation to 7 percent by late 1978. With several years of additional stimulus, say 8 percent M_1 growth, inflation could be pushed up to within hailing distance of double-digit figures.

Even if the Federal Reserve permitted M_1 to grow at the bottom of its target range, inflation would remain at 6 percent for several years. We are locked in by the 10-quarter uniformly weighted lag and last year's unusual 7 percent M_1 growth. (See Section 6.3.)

(4) By virtue of the uniformly distributed 10-quarter lag, sharp changes in M_1 growth for several quarters in either direction will have little effect on current inflation. Even large quarterly M_1 growth deviations from the M_1 growth trend will have little effect on inflation as long as they average out to the prescribed trend value within about four quarters (see Section 6.5). For purposes of stabilizing inflation at some specified trend value, it is sufficient to require that quarterly M_1 growth out average to the associated M_1 growth trend every four quarters. For inflation watchers, it is the trend, not short-term M_1 movements, that counts.

(5) The satisfactory 1976-1977 forecasting performance of the M_1 model, estimated on the basis of a pre-1971 sample period, infers that the recently observed shift in the heretofore stable demand for money equation, an important facet of monetarism, should not be explained in terms of significant changes in the payments mechanism. (See Section 3.5.) Had there been significant economizing of money, we would expect the M_1 model to progressively underforecast inflation.

(6) The stability of the M_1-price elasticity over more than 20 years and the relative stability of the constant term used to capture the trend effects of the real sector on the price level suggest considerable stability in the dynamics of price determination on the aggregate level. Additional evidence is the quick recovery, beginning in 1976, of the simulation forecasts that were begun in mid-1971; however, the presence of the 1974-1975 recession somewhat clouds matters.

(7) The estimated 1.4 M_1-price elasticity does not shed any direct light on whether the quantity theory holds in the short run owing to the highly aggregated manner in which output and velocity effects on the price level were treated in the trend term. Indeed, the model falls apart when the trend term (constant) is constrained to zero; this type of model is too simple to resolve the issue. However, the slightly greater than 1 value of the M_1-price elasticity and the negative coefficient for the trend term (capturing the net consequences on the price level from output and velocity effects) are at least consistent with a short-run quantity theory.

1.5 Accounting for Unexplained Inflation: 1973-1975

While the M_1 model does a good job explaining inflation over the last two decades solely in terms of money growth and a trend variable capturing net output and velocity effects on the price level, it does fail to explain 4 percent of the 33 percent increase in the price level between late 1973 and 1975. To be sure, there is a long list of suggested causes for the near doubling in inflation between late 1973 and 1974: the quadruple oil price hike, sharp increase in primary commodity prices, dollar devaluation, adoption of floating exchange rates, agricultural production shortfalls, synchronization of aggregate demand among the industrialized economies, and so on. While explaining the origin of that inflation surge is not the principal focus of the study, it does have an important bearing on the relevance of the monetarist inflation thesis. Chapter 5 is concerned with this issue.

It is quite clear that the M_1 model *cannot* be extended with the addition of a variable or two for the purposes of econometrically explaining the 1973-1975 inflation surge. The highly aggregated single-equation approach used in this study is simply too clumsy to econometrically explain with any degree of confidence the origins of the 4 percent in increase in the price level that cannot be accounted for by money growth and the trend variable. A multiequation or input/output approach is more sensible.

Nonetheless, the 1971/3-1975 forecast errors do provide the basis for rich noneconometric insights about the sources of nonmonetary inflation. Not only can valuable insights about the effects of controls, the oil shock, primary commodity price increases, and the synchronized expansion explanation be obtained, but a suggestive scenario for the post 1973/4 inflation surge can be presented that fits into the highly aggregative monetarist framework used for explaining changes in the price level. The forecast errors are certainly unusual in that they sequentially appear in two separate groups, one individually over forecasting inflation, the other individually underforecasting inflation.

Between 1971/3 and 1973/1 or roughly corresponding with Phases I and II of wage/price controls, the simulation *overforecasts* inflation by about 2 percentage points. This overforecast is properly interpreted as an estimate of the controls' suppression effect and closely agrees with estimates by econometric studies of controls (See Section 5.4a). Furthermore, prior to the quadruple oil price hike quarter, 1973/4, the simulation suggests that there is no "foreign influence" on United States inflation; for a half-year prior to this quarter, the forecasts were accurate. If there was a foreign influence on United States inflation, it must have been imported between 1973/4 and late 1975.

An unusual feature of the simulation is that the forecast errors closely parallel the inflation surge from 1973/4 to 1974/4 and the abrupt deceleration in 1975/2. In the oil price hike quarter, 1973/4, inflation and the forecast errors both increase by 2 percentage points. By 1974/4, both have increased 5 percentage points over their 1973/3 values of 7 and 0 percent, respectively. Two quarters later, in 1975/2, they both abruptly decline by 5 percentage points, and a half-year later the simulation is again tracking satisfactorily.

The simulation suggests that the sharp increase in nonoil primary commodity prices in 1973-1974 did *not* significantly affect United States inflation. The evidence is as follows. The parallel 5-quarter acceleration and subsequent deceleration in inflation and the forecast errors are closely paralleled by various IMF dollar-denominated nonoil primary commodity export price indices.[22] Yet in the 1976-1977 period, the IMF series have generally surpassed their previous 1974 peaks, but the simulation is forecasting quite nicely *solely* in terms of money growth and the trend factor. Since the nonoil primary commodity price cycle is repeating itself without *any* evidence of nonmonetary price effects other than those captured by the trend factor, it is reasonable to draw the inference that the earlier price cycle was not responsible for a significant portion of the 1973-1974 inflation surge. Input/output studies of the cost push pass through by Cagan and Berner, Clark, Enzler, and Lowrey reached a similar conclusion.[23] (See Section 5.4c.)

In using the Pierce/Enzler and Gordon econometric estimates that the direct oil price effects lasted only about three quarters, the inference drawn from the forecast errors (for the 1973/4-1974/2 period) is that at a maximum the direct consequences of the oil price hike raised the price level by 1 to 1.5 percent.[24] This maximum figure is well below the Pierce/Enzler and Gordon estimates, but is in line with the Project Link studies.[25]

A tentative explanation of the surge and subsequent collapse in inflation and the forecasting errors, between 1973/4 and 1975, is as follows. Prior to the oil price hike, the forecast errors imply a significant 2 percent price suppression effect from wage/price controls but no evidence of any foreign influence on United States inflation. Now, it is reasonable to suppose that the controls' suppression effect was subsequently reversed, but the forecast errors clearly imply this did *not* happen *prior to* 1973/4. The oil shock was imposed on an economy that had been expanding for two prior years and was about to begin a major price adjustment, reversing the controls' price suppression. Indeed, the reversal and money growth together were sufficient to generate almost 9 percent average inflation in 1974. Given the peculiar circumstances of an economy enjoying a sustained expansion and poised to recoup the suppression effects from wage/price controls, the oil shock generated an expectation-based surge in *excess demand* manifesting itself in materials stockpiling and hoarding. However, the oil shock also precipitated a severe recession in the industrialized economies. After a year of declining real output, it was apparent in early 1975 that there was no underlying aggregate demand supporting the expectation-based excess demand for goods and materials.[26] Excess demand collapsed in 1975/2.

Several features of this scenario are as follows. First, while the 1973/4-1974 forecast errors imply that nonmonetary effects other than those captured by the trend factor are increasing the price level, the subsequent errors do not indicate the presence of any effects working in the *reverse* direction to reduce any portion of the previous unexplained increase in the price level. This suggests that the inflation surge did not originate in the synchronized expansion of the industrial economies. After all, the subsequent contraction was also synchronized and far more severe, yet there was no evidence that any of the previous increase in the price level was reversed. Second, the major factors behind the surge also explain the sudden collapse in inflation in 1975/2. The oil cost push pass through was a one-time effect lasting about three quarters.[27] The controls reversal was also a one-time effect. And the surge in excess demand could not be expected to continue in the face of declining aggregate real output. Third, the sudden surge and the subsequent collapse in inflation with the lasting effects on the price level being a 4 percent permanent increase suggest a stable aggregate price mechanism, supporting the monetarists' view of a stable private sector.

1.6 Policy Recommendation

The principal policy recommendation from this study of the monetarist inflation thesis is that to make any serious progress toward price stability, the uncharacteristically high M_1 growth rates of the 1970s must be substantially lowered by the Federal Reserve. The length of time required to achieve price stability is sufficiently long as to require, at least temporarily, a major change in the way monetary policy is conducted in the United States. Since we are in a mature phase of the present business cycle expansion, there is the danger that it may take as long as a decade to achieve the price stability characteristic of the 1950s. The effect of the monetary impulse upon the price level is sufficiently delayed that unless a lower M_1 growth program is begun with dispatch, we may be in danger of institutionalizing 6 percent inflation.

It is clear that restoration of even moderate price stability, 1.5 to 2.5 percent inflation, cannot be quickly achieved. (See Section 6.4.) Even under a crash program of immediately "biting the bullet" and adopting 2 percent M_1 growth, there would be little visible progress. Inflation would average 5 percent in the first year of such a program, not far removed from our current 6 percent figure, and about 2.5 years would be required to realize price stability. A more sensible program that is much less likely to impose temporary adjustments on the economy calls for a phased annual reduction in M_1 growth rate by about 1 percent per year.

Under a 1 percent per annum M_1 growth reduction, M_1 growth would be reduced to 6 percent in 1978, 5 percent in 1979, 4 percent in 1980, and so on. This program would require about five years for completion. However, under the first two years, inflation would continue to remain at 6 percent, reflecting the delayed impact of 1977's 7 percent M_1 growth. Progress would be slow, indeed. Our only requirement is that the Federal Reserve *average* M_1 growth to preselected rates each year during the course of the program. Given the length of the lag of M_1 growth upon inflation, no restrictions on quarterly M_1 growth rates need be imposed other than yearly average target figures.

If such a program were mandated, the obvious political difficulty is that it would require temporarily putting aside the conventional pursuit of countercyclical monetary policy. Since we are in a mature phase of the business cycle (March 1975 was the trough) and 1980 is election year, the opportunities for adding additional monetary stimulus to the economy would be denied. Ideally, the "opportune" time with which to implement a phased M_1 growth reduction program is during an economic expansion; however, the length of time, about five years, that it would take to complete the program is fairly long in relation to average postwar business cycle expansions.

From a monetarist perspective, there is a peculiar irony about the phased M_1 growth-reduction anti-inflation program. The Federal Reserve, left to pursue conventional monetary policy in its own wisdom, has given us almost a decade of 6 percent average M_1 growth. One result of that policy has been 6 percent inflation. However, the time over which the monetary impulse affects the price level is sufficiently long, 2.5 years to be exact, that any serious program to bring about price stability requires the suspension of countercyclical monetary policy for half a decade, subject, of course, to unforeseen contingencies. One special benefit from following that program is that it would provide valuable insight on the monetarists' contention that the inherent stability of the private economy contrasts with the destabilizing influence of a varying monetary impulse. If the phased M_1 growth-reduction program supports this view, we might want to consider further restrictions on the conduct of monetary policy in the United States.

The other side of the coin is that a phased M_1 growth-reduction anti-inflation program may conflict with the other goals of monetary policy. Our study clearly does not provide insights on the policy tradeoffs issue, but even a cursory glance at the real output and unemployment figures over the previous decade while M_1 growth was jacked up suggests that high M_1 growth was not especially successful in those pursuits either. Since we have strong evidence of a causal M_1 growth-inflation link, the shoe is on the other foot, so to speak. It is the obligation of others, and especially the Federal Reserve, to argue persuasively why a M_1 growth-reduction program is not in the interests of our economic well-being. With that perspective, the following proposal is recommended.

Proposal: Congress should require that the Federal Reserve System immediately begin a phased M_1 growth-reduction program by about 1 percent per year until M_1 growth is brought down to a rate consistent with price stability, about 2 percent per annum. To aid the adjustment process, this policy should be publicly announced together with an agenda of expected yearly average M_1 growth rates required to complete the program's goals.

The organization of the study is as follows. In Chapter 2 the model used to test the thesis is detailed and the econometric testing procedures are carefully explained. In Chapter 3 the first part of the thesis is rigorously examined for the most popular money definition, M_1. In Chapter 4 the analysis is replicated, but on a lesser scale for M_2, M_3, total reserves, nonborrowed reserves, reserve base, and Niehans's specification. Chapter 5 examines the second part of the thesis with the correctly specified M_1 monetarist inflation model and discusses at some length the unusually interesting set of forecast errors. The policy implications of the study together with a variety of post-1978 inflation forecasts out to 1981 are presented in Chapter 6.

Notes

1. Recent surveys of the scholarly literature include D.E.W. Laidler and J.M. Parkin, "Inflation—A Survey," *The Economic Journal*, no. 340 (December 1975): 741-809; R. Gordon, "Recent Developments in the Theory of Inflation and Unemployment," *Journal of Monetary Economics* 2, no. 2 (April 1976): 185-220; H. Frisch, "Inflation Theory 1963-1975: A Second Generation 'Survey,' " *Journal of Economic Literature* 15, no. 4 (December 1977).

2. M. Friedman, *The Counter Revolution in Monetary Theory* (London: Institute of Economic Affairs for Wincott Foundation, 1970), Occasional paper No. 33, p. 24.

3. For example, see R. Gordon, "Can the Inflation of the 1970's Be Explained?" *BPEA* 1(1977): 256-76.

4. Ibid.

5. See note 1 in Chapter 5 for references.

6. On monetarism see T. Mayer, "The Structure of Monetarism, I and II," *Kredit and Kapital* (April and July 1975): 190-218 and 293-316, also reprinted in *The Structure of Monetarism* (New York: W.W. Norton, forthcoming); A.R. Nobay and H. Johnson, "Monetarism: A Historic-Theoretic Perspective," *Journal of Economic Literature* 15, no. 2 (June 1977): 470-85; H. Johnson, "The Keynesian Revolution and the Monetarist Counter-revolution," *American Economic Review* 61, no. 2 (May 1977): 1-14, reprinted in H. Johnson, *On Economics and Society* (Chicago:

University of Chicago Press, 1975), pp. 91-106; M. Friedman, "The Role of Monetary Policy," *American Economic Review* 58, no. 1 (March 1969): 1-17, reprinted in M. Friedman, *The Optimum Quantity of Money and Other Essays* (Chicago: Aldine, 1969), pp. 95-110; J. Stein, "The Monetarist Criticism of the New Economics," in J. Stein (ed.) *Monetarism* (North Holland, 1976), pp. 1-16.

7. K. Brunner, "The Role of Money and Monetary Policy," *Review* of the Federal Reserve Bank of St. Louis, July 1968, pp. 8-24.

8. For monetarists, *thee* challenge, see Stein, "The Monetarist Criticism of the New Economics."

9. Mayer, "The Structure of Monetarism, I and II."

10. M. Friedman, "The Quantity Theory—A Restatement," in M. Friedman, *Studies in the Quantity Theory of Money* (Chicago: University of Chicago Press, 1956); Friedman, "Role of Monetary Policy"; M. Friedman and A. Schwartz, *A Monetary History of the United States* (Princeton University for NBER, 1963); K. Brunner and A. Meltzer, "Money, Debt and Economic Activity," *Journal of Political Economy* 80, no. 5 (September/October 1972): 951-77.

11. Nobay and Johnson, "Monetarism: A Historic-Theoretic Perspective."

12. A. Schwartz, "Secular Price Change in Historical Perspective," *Journal of Money, Credit and Banking* 5, no. 1, Part II (February 1973): 243-69.

13. Frisch, "Inflation Theory 1963-1975," p. 1298.

14. Stein, "Monetarist Criticism of the New Economics."

15. L. Andersen and D. Karnosky, "The Appropriate Time Frame for Controlling Monetary Aggregates: The St. Louis Evidence," *Controlling Monetary Aggregates II: The Implementation*, Conference Series No. 9 (Federal Reserve Bank of Boston, September 1972); D. Karnosky, "The Link between Money and Prices: 1971-76," *Review* of the Federal Reserve Bank of St. Louis, June 1976, pp. 17-23.

16. See Mayer, "Structure of Monetarism, I and II," for a good discussion on this point.

17. For a good example of a single-equation monetarist model, see D. Dutton, "Economics of Inflation and Output Fluctuations in the United States, 1952-74," *Journal of Monetary Economics*, 1978, forthcoming.

18. C. Sims, "Money Income and Causality," *American Economic Review* 62, no. 4 (September 1972): 540-52; C.W.J. Granger, "Investigating Causal Relations by Econometric Models and Cross-Spectral Methods," *Econometrica* 37, no. 3 (July 1969): 424-38.

19. Andersen and Karnosky, "Appropriate Time Frame for Controlling Money Aggregates," and Karnosky, "Link between Money and Prices."

20. Not an unexpected result. See E. Fiege and D. Pearce, "The Substitutability of Money and Near Monies: A Survey of the Time-Series Evidence," *Journal of Economic Literature* 15, no. 2 (June 1977): 439-69.

21. J. Niehans, "How to Fill an Empty Shell," *American Economic Review*, May 1976, pp. 177-83.

22. L. Goreau, "The Use of Compensatory Financing," *Finance and Development* 14, no. 3 (September 1977): 20-24.

23. P. Cagan, *The Effect of World Prices on U.S. Inflation* (New York: NBER, 1977), multilith. R. Berner, P. Clark, J. Enzler, and B. Lowrey, "International Sources of Domestic Inflation," Joint Economic Committee *Studies in Price Stability and Economic Growth*, 94th Cong., 1st Sess., August 1975.

24. J. Pierce and J. Enzler, "The Effects of External Inflationary Shocks," *BPEA* 1(1974): 13-54; R. Gordon, "The Impact of Demand on Prices," *BPEA* 3(1975): 613-62.

25. J. Waelbroeck (ed.), *The Models of Project Link* (North Holland, 1976).

26. The output effects are clearly shown in Pierce and Enzler, "Effects of External Inflationary Shocks," for the United States economy.

27. Pierce and Enzler, ibid.; Gordon, "Impact of Demand on Prices."

2 A Procedure for Testing the Monetarist Inflation Thesis

2.1 Introduction and Overview

This chapter will describe the model, analytical methods, and standards of evidence used in this econometric study of the monetarist inflation thesis. Recall that for our study the thesis is defined as two propositions. First, there is a stable, causal, and powerful relationship between money growth and inflation. Second, money growth has remained the predominant source of inflation even during the 1970s. To test the first part, the strategy is to carefully estimate the model identified in this study as a monetarist inflation model with the sample period running from the mid-1950s through mid-1971 (the onset of wage/price controls). To test the second part of the thesis, the successful model(s) estimated on the basis of a pre-1971 sample period is forward-simulated from mid-1971 to date, late 1977.

The model used is a shifting distributed lag quasi-reduced form of money growth on inflation where an unusual, but not unreasonable, provision is made for the effects of changes in real aggregate output and velocity upon the price level. The main driving force is the gradual adjustment of current inflation to past money growth incorporated in a distributed lag. The output and velocity effects on the price level are aggregated and are represented by a constant that functions as a growth term. This constant, or growth term, is not expected to remain stable over long periods; however, the model's viability is contingent on some degree of stability for this term.

The features of this deceptively simple model are that it readily facilitates testing causality required to establish evidence for the exogeneity assumption, focuses on the stability of the money-price elasticity, and facilitates forward simulation for testing the second part of the thesis and examining a variety of money specifications. On the other hand, the highly aggregated manner in which the output and velocity effects on the price level are treated suggests that the model will be unstable. Since the money-price relationship is incorporated in a distributed lag, the ordinarily difficult task of correctly estimating distributed lags is compounded inasmuch as the model can be expected to shift over time. It is important to note that this highly aggregated model will prove insufficient to test whether the quantity theory of prices holds in the short term, owing to the rather rough treatment of the output and velocity effects. Furthermore, the risks with this model are one-sided; strong results provide positive support for the thesis, while ambiguous results may not be meaningful.

Since in a real sense this study is an econometric investigation of whether any of the conventional definitions of money can be properly specified with respect to causality, stability, and adjustment pattern in the model used to represent the monetarist inflation thesis, there is a premium on maintaining a high econometric standard. In this chapter a specific testing procedure, including estimation methods and analytical techniques, is carefully outlined. In the remaining portion of the study, the results of carrying out that procedure, warts and all, are presented. The entire evidence is made available so that "quality" relative to the merits of the tests procedure can be readily evaluated.

The scope of our econometric inquiry is briefly indicated below.

(1) In addition to the three conventional broad monetary aggregates—M_1, M_2, and M_3 (and by inference M_4 and M_5)—three "high-powered money" or reserve aggregates are examined: total member bank reserves, nonborrowed member bank reserves, and the reserve base. While not all candidates would be expected to be suitable specifications in monetarist inflation models, the totality of the evidence warrants close inspection. It matters greatly, for example, if M_2 is unsuitable simply because it gives poor results or because its demand and time/savings deposit components have different relationships with inflation. Perhaps our minimum expectations are some support from both a broad aggregate, especially M_1, and a reserve aggregate.

(2) Econometric testing of unidirectional causality between money growth and inflation is a major facet of our study. A sizable portion of the econometric estimation resources available to this study will be used to test causality between inflation and the growth in M_1, M_2, time/savings deposits at commercial banks, and total reserves. Unless the evidence supports the claimed causality direction, estimations of distributed lag models are unreliable. In this study the procedure developed by Sims for testing the widely accepted Granger definition of causality between a pair of time series is used. The Sims procedure employs distributed lag time-series regressions, makes careful use of the *F* test, and is subject to all the usual problems of carefully estimating distributed lags. The causality tests provide important and necessary evidence on whether the monetarist inflation thesis forms the basis for a sensible modeling of inflation. To be sure, such evidence will not necessarily convince those skeptical about the hypothesized causality running from changes in money growth to changes in inflation, but at least the evidence will be available for review.

(3) To attempt a high econometric standard, extensive use is made of five sensitivity testing procedures—lengthening sample, backward lengthening sample, overlapping sample, straddle, and sideways straddle—together

with out-of-sample forward simulations. Those tests are described in Section 2.3b. Most of the approximately 200 estimations in this study use the Almon method (third-degree polynomial specification) simply because it enables intensive sensitivity analysis to be made with relatively small samples. The preferred Shiller method is used to reestimate the more promising estimations, and a check is also made with OLS. While it is always in order to use other estimation methods, they were not readily available. The peculiar nature of the distributed lags and the equivalence of the Shiller and Almon estimations for the model identified in this study as correct suggest that these findings are not estimation-dependent. Finally, rather strong standards of statistical significance and stability for distributed lag models are used. A model is considered significant (and stable) when *each* one of its estimated individual distributed lag coefficients is significant (and stable) rather than merely their sum.

The appropriate sample period for estimating monetarist inflation models should, insofar as possible, abstract from major nonmonetary inflation influences. These effects are nonmonetary in the sense that we would not expect money growth alone to capture their influence on the price level. We selected the mid-1950s to mid-1971. The initial sample point reflects the combined influence of the Korean war and the Treasury-Federal Reserve "accord" in early 1951. The endpoint reflects the onset of wage/price controls in August 1971. Important econometric evidence does exist that wage/price controls significantly suppressed the price level until late 1972. Thereafter, an almost bewildering variety of mostly interrelated nonmonetary explanations have been suggested to explain the inflation surge. They include, for example, the quadruple OPEC oil price hike, sharp increases in prices of primary commodities, grain production shortfalls, dollar devaluation, floating exchange rates, and synchronization of demand in the industrialized economies.

If, as observers suggest, the post-1971 period does contain major nonmonetary price effects, then we have a good period with which to test whether money growth continues to remain the major determinant of inflation. To support the thesis, a monetarist inflation model that satisfactorily explains pre-1971 inflation should give satisfactory inflation forecasts beginning, say, in late 1975. Also, if the monetary influence predominated, then the net influence of all the post-1971 nonmonetary price effects together should be a permanent rise in the price level by an amount less than the average inflation predicted for this period on the basis of money growth.

In concluding this introduction and overview, it is important to explicitly state the standards that, in the author's opinion, would constitute strong (and therefore meaningful) econometric evidence supporting the monetarist inflation thesis.

(1) Inflation should be satisfactorily, but not necessarily completely, explained by at least one econometrically robust monetarist inflation model from the mid- to late 1950s to mid-1971. The money-price *elasticity* should be *stable*. Also, the model(s) should satisfactorily forecast inflation beginning, say, in late 1975. For the other specifications, there should be reasonable empirical explanations why they are not satisfactory.

(2) For those models otherwise econometrically valid, the Sims test of Granger causality should support unidirectional causality running from changes in money growth to changes in inflation.

(3) The net effect of unexplained post-1971 inflation should be a permanent rise in the price level by an amount less than the average inflation predicted by money growth for that period. The monetary influence on inflation, then, should be the predominant one for the past two decades.

The organization of the chapter is as follows. First, the specification of the general monetarist inflation model used in this study to test the thesis is discussed in Section 2.2. Then the econometric problems associated with distributed lag models are briefly described in Section 2.3, and a suggested test procedure is detailed. A brief discussion of the requirements for a Sims test of Granger causality follows in Section 2.4. Last, the procedure for testing predominance of monetary over nonmonetary inflation in the 1970s is outlined in Section 2.5.

2.2 Specifying the Monetarist Inflation Model

In the broad aggregative framework used by monetarists, changes in the monetary impulse generated by the monetary authorities induce major changes in aggregate demand which ultimately are allocated between changes in aggregate output and the price level.[1] Since the dynamic short-run adjustment of the price level and real output to the monetary disturbance is held to occur both jointly and simultaneously, the thesis should be ideally tested within a model that fully accounts for the dynamic adjustments to the monetary impulse.[2] It will not do to study the short-run dynamic adjustments of the price level to the monetary impulse and ignore the other parts of the adjustment process. However, since the details of the transmission mechanism whereby the impulse ultimately affects the price level and aggregate output in the monetarist framework have been neither sufficiently "fleshed out" nor agreed upon, the thesis must be tested with an incomplete model.[3]

a. The General Monetarist Inflation Model

The approach used here is to keep the modeling as simple as possible and work within a single-equation reduced-form type of framework. Since causality testing between money growth and inflation is such an important issue and causality tests require pairwise testing, a reduced-form equation is appropriate. With a more ambitious model, causality testing would still require access to a reduced form of money growth on inflation. Since the dynamic adjustment of the price level to past money growth in the monetarist framework is a gradual one extending over several years, the natural modeling for the dynamic adjustment uses distributed lags. Since we want to cast a broad net and examine a range of money specifications rather than narrowly focus on M_1, a single-equation distributed lag helps keep the estimation task within reasonable bounds. And to test the second part of the thesis—predominance of monetary inflation in the 1970s-dynamic forward simulation is required. It is a convenience for this purpose, too, to keep the model as simple as possible.

The problem in modeling the adjustment of the price level to the monetary impulse is accommodating the effects of changes in real output upon the price level and any changes in the velocity of circulation. By inference, the monetarist inflation thesis implies a powerful and stable relationship between changes in the price level and the monetary impulse. If this is true, then the *net* consequence of all other effects on inflation will not be a major determinant of changes in the price level and can be approximated by a constant term. This is not to suggest that short-run changes in output do not have important effects on the price level, only that when all nonmonetary effects on the price level are lumped together, they will not be a significant source of variation in the price level. In this formulation, then, inflation is determined by changes in money growth together with a constant term designed to capture the trend effect on inflation from changes in output and velocity.

Whether this formulation will be satisfactory remains to be seen, but it does place primary emphasis on the stability and explanatory power of the money growth-inflation relationship. If the "other" effects are an important source of short-run changes in the price level, this formulation will not work. But if they can be roughly captured by a trend term, the simple model will achieve its purpose. It is important to note that this type of modeling will be insufficient to test whether the quantity theory holds in the short run, i.e. that changes in the money supply are proportional to changes in the price level. The estimated elasticity will be biased inasmuch as the effects of changes in output upon the price level induced by the monetary impulse are captured by the constant term. This is not a serious drawback since our principal purpose is to focus on the stability and explanatory power of the money growth-inflation relationship. Also, note that the constant would not be expected to remain stable over long periods. But in order for the model to be estimated, it cannot be highly unstable. Finally, should a simple model described above prove unsatisfactory, the thesis may not suffer much damage. But if there is strong empirical support from this simple modeling, then the thesis does merit support.

Taking our cue from the well-known quantity identity in terms of velocity (v), money supply (m), price (p), and real output (q), all expressed in growth rates, we have

$$p + q = m + v \tag{2.1}$$

Using functional notation, our model is expressed as follows:

$$p = f(m) + g(v,q) + u \tag{2.2}$$

where u is the stochastic term and $g(v,q)$ is also a function of m in recognition that the monetary impulse in the short run affects both the price level and real output. The crucial *assumption* is that $g(v,q)$ can be approximated by a fairly stable constant term. Since both the price level and the money supply are expressed in growth rates, that constant is a growth term, capturing the inflation associated with the *net* consequences of changes in real output and velocity. Simplifying, we have

$$p = f(m) + a + v \tag{2.3}$$

where a is used to approximate $g(v,q)$ and v is a stochastic term. We will refer to Equation (2.3) as the "monetarist inflation model" in our study.

Equation (2.3) can be referred to as a shifting quasi-reduced-form distributed lag model where $f(m)$ is represented by a distributed lag of money growth on inflation and the constant is allowed to shift from time to time. Naturally, if the constant is shifting fairly often, the model cannot be estimated by conventional techniques. The model is only a quasi-reduced form, owing to the rather rough treatment given the output and velocity effects on the price level embodied in the constant term. While $f(m)$ can be considered exogenous to p (subject to causality testing), a cannot be so considered and, not being a variable, cannot be subjected to causality tests. The expected sign of a should be small and negative. By holding v fixed, then for a given monetary impulse an increase in q will reduce p. Similarly, by holding q fixed, then for a given monetary impulse an increase in v will increase p. If the effect of q, as seems likely, is stronger than the effect of v, then a will be negative. Given the heroic role of a, the money-price elasticity may or may not be greater than 1, but it should certainly be positive for M_1 and neither very large nor very small.

The complete form of the general monetarist inflation model used in this study is expressed as follows:

$$p_t = a + \sum_{i=0}^{n} w_i m_{t-i} + v \qquad (2.4)$$

where p_t and m_t are expressed in annualized growth rates, t denotes the time period (e.g. quarters), n denotes the number of distributed lags, the w_i are the weights or distributed lag coefficients, and v is a stochastic term assumed normally distributed with zero expectation. Also, m is assumed exogenous with respect to p; this assumption requires causality testing.

Since both p and m are expressed as growth rates, i.e. inflation and money growth, the sum of the distributed lag coefficients is properly interpreted as the money-price *elasticity.* Considerable attention will be given to the stability of this term. Also, note that with n distributed lags, there are $n + 1$ lag coefficients or weights where w_0 refers to the current period. The principal features of the model are the stability and estimated values of the distributed lag coefficients, the length of lag, and the stability and value of the constant term. For any given specifications of p and m, there are an infinite number of possible lag distributions. From this perspective, the econometric effort is designed to examine whether for any of the usual specifications of money, Equation (2.4) can be properly specified as to both the distributed lag and the causality requirements.

The model expressed in Equation (2.4) has been used by Andersen and Karnosky to demonstrate that there is a direct money-price link.[4] Others have also found it tempting.[5] However, the half-dozen or so estimations of this model that have come to the author's attention were offered without any supporting sensitivity analysis, specification analysis with money definitions other than M_1, or causality analysis confirming the exogeneity assumption. More important than ignoring the usual econometric prerequisites is that the *spirit* in which Equation (2.4) is offered be quite different from how it has been used by others. No mention is made in these other studies of the *unusual* role of the constant term and the importance of testing its stability. Nor is there any discussion of whether the estimated elasticity values are biased. Not surprisingly, the elasticity estimates vary, as do the lag lengths. Virtue has its own reward, however; it is easy to show in Section 3.2 that these previous estimations are incorrect.

b. Specifying the Monetary Aggregate

If we were restricted to just one choice of defining money, it would be M_1. We do have evidence that the cross-price elasticities between M_1 and the near monies are inelastic.[6] However, since the thesis does not define money and economists do not have a consensus on the "correct" definition of money, the pragmatic approach is to econometrically examine the more common definitions and review the evidence.[7] Such a procedure makes for a long study, but it is precisely because empirical relationships involving money are known to be sensitive to how money is specified that it is important to cast a broad net and inspect the evidence.[8] If only one definition leads to an econometrically reliable monetarist inflation model (as defined in our study) with the other definitions simply giving implausible results, few are likely to be impressed. Furthermore, a priori, there is no strong reason to expect that any particular definition is "correct" except perhaps with respect to M_1, or that empirically successful definitions yield consistent models.

The most common definitions are the broad monetary aggregates: M_1, M_2, and M_3. M_1 consists of the public's holdings of currency and their demand deposits (checkbook money) at banks. M_2 adds to M_1 the time/savings deposits at commercial banks [excluding large negotiable certificates of deposit (CDs)]. M_3 adds to M_2 the time/saving deposits at thrift institutions (savings and loan associations, mutual savings banks, and credit unions). M_3 also excludes large negotiable CDs. The M_4 and M_5 definitions add back the large negotiable CDs to M_2 and M_3, respectively. For each of the three basic aggregates, the Federal Reserve has posted growth targets since 1975, although M_1 receives the lion's share of attention.[9] While each of these specifications is useful, the most likely candidate is M_1 simply because M_2 and M_3 (M_4 and M_5, also) contain non-interest-bearing demand deposits in addition to their major components, interest-earning time/savings deposits. A priori, it is not clear that interest-earning and non-interest-earning deposits should have the same inflation response, or if the responses are different but econometrically reliable, whether their combined effect can be correctly captured in a monetarist inflation model specifying a broader monetary aggregate.

We also need to examine "high-powered" money or (loosely) reserve balances held by member banks against deposit liabilities. Roughly the banking system can expand deposits up to a multiple of available reserve balances. Control over the money supply is usually exercised by controlling the amount of reserve balances available to banks and hence is indirect by virtue of our fractional reserve banking system. A frequent view is that the money stock can be controlled by the Federal Reserve (if it chooses to do so) for periods of at least a quarter of a year.[10]

Three commonly used reserve specifications are total reserves, nonborrowed reserves, and the reserve base. Total reserves include member bank deposits at the Federal Reserve and bank vault cash holding. Nonborrowed reserves excludes from total reserves those borrowed from the Federal Reserve. The reserve base adds the public's currency holdings to total reserves. Reserves are often used as a measure of monetary policy in simulations with large econometric models.[11] Since the broad monetary aggregates are linked to the monetary reserve aggregates by the money multiplier, it would be reasonable to expect that if a broad aggregate is a suitable specification, then one of the reserve aggregates should also give promising results. Finally, Niehans has recently suggested yet another monetary measure, the size of the Federal Reserve's government securities portfolio, and this, too, deserves a brief look.[12]

While it is clear that a specification problem exists with respect to the independent variable, it is not obvious that no problems arise in specifying the price level. For a broad-based indicator of price-level changes, the implicit GNP price deflator is clearly preferred to the CPI and WPI, both of which have limited coverage and involve double counting of price changes. However, the GNP deflator does include the influence from "foreign" factors, and the gross private domestic product (GPDP) deflator might be preferred. As a practical matter, quarterly changes of the GNP and GPDP deflators are virtually perfectly correlated; for purposes of estimating monetarist inflation models, differences between the series cannot be discriminated. (See Section 3.6c.) Specifying the price level is less of a problem than for money since there are fewer alternatives.

c. *Time Specification*

A priori, it is not clear what is the suitable period over which changes in the price level and the money supply should be computed. If a valid relationship does exist, then as time is divided more finely, ultimately we will reach a point where the relationship does not hold. And, as the interval for computing growth rates is extended, the distributed lag may not be correctly estimated. For example, with a true lag of 1.5 years, annual growth figures will be inadequate.

As a practical matter, the implicit GNP price deflator is available on a quarterly basis; a demanding sensitivity analysis of distributed lags, when confined to the post-Korean war period (see Section 2.2d) requires a sizable number of observations, feasible only with quarterly data. Promising results will be rechecked with semiannual growth rate figures. It would have been desirable to use unadjusted money stock figures, but this is not a serious omission.[13]

Since the usual way of forming series of annualized quarterly growth rate figures is to use the transformation $\Delta \log 400$, the general monetarist inflation model used in this study can be rewritten as follows:

$$\Delta \log p_t \cdot 400 = a + \sum_{i=0}^{n} w_i \Delta \log m_{t-i} \cdot 400 + v \qquad (2.5)$$

Note that the weights, w_i, can be directly translated into percentage points. For example, if w_0 is 0.1, then a 1 percent increase in the current quarter's money growth rate would increase inflation by 0.1 percentage point. Also note that when referring to inflation in this study, we use the terms *percent* and *percentage point*; for our purposes, they are equivalent, and the latter one is used on occasion to avoid any confusion. Also since inflation is defined here as growth of the price level, the phrase *rate of inflation* is not used, for that would refer to the second derivative.

d. Sample Period Selection

To properly estimate Equation (2.5), the sample period should be restricted to those times relatively free of unusual nonmonetary price effects. The only mechanism for capturing the influence of these effects is the constant term (the trend factor). If this term is sufficiently unstable or even moderately unstable, then our simple model will not be able to be estimated with conventional techniques. Conceptually, if we had a more detailed model, more powerful estimation techniques, and specific knowledge of the unusual nonmonetary price effects, then we could be somewhat indifferent to sample period selection. Given the limitations of our approach, it is fairly clear that mid-1971, with the onset of wage/price controls, should be the sample endpoint. We do have important econometric evidence that inflation was significantly suppressed by about 2 percent during the first six quarters of controls, i.e. Phases I and II. (See Section 5.4c.) Subsequently, a veritable host of unusual nonmonetary price effects have been suggested as partially responsible for explaining the unusual behavior of the price level in 1973-1975. On many lists would be included the quadruple oil price hike, sharp increases in primary commodities, synchronized expansion among the industrial economies, agricultural production shortfalls, devaluation of the dollar, and adoption of floating exchange rates. (See Section 5.4.) Indeed, it is the very existence of this list that poses an important challenge to the monetarist inflation thesis. Recall that an important test of the thesis requires that a monetarist inflation model which fairly successfully explains pre-1970 inflation be available for forward-simulation purposes through the 1970s.

While the appropriate sample endpoint is determined by the onset of wage/price controls in August 1971, the initial sample point can be fixed only approximately. Several years are needed to maintain a reasonable distance from the effects of the Korean war on the price level; otherwise, an intolerable burden is placed upon our simple model. Also, the model hypothesizes that money growth is exogenous with respect to changes in the price level. An independent postwar monetary policy slowly evolved after the March 1951 Treasury-Federal Reserve "accord" when the Federal Reserve announced it would no longer circumscribe monetary policy, e.g. open market activities, to pegging interest rates on government securities.[14] Perhaps the adoption of the "bills only" policy by the Federal Reserve in March 1953 marks the approximate beginning of an independent postwar monetary policy. Since "independent" money growth data, reflecting purposeful Federal Reserve policy, are required if money growth is considered exogenous with respect to inflation, the initial sample point permitting the estimation of the *complete* distributed lag should begin several years later, depending upon the lag length. For example, a 1956 or 1957 initial sample point would be suitable for a three-year distributed lag. In using 1956 as the initial sample point and a five-year lag, the first quarter's money growth that enters into the estimation is 1951/1. The appropriate sample period for estimating Equation (2.5) is the mid-1950s through mid-1971.

2.3 Estimating Distributed Lag Models

The empirical part of our study is largely concerned with carefully estimating the distributed lag model described in Equation (2.5). Since we expect that the constant term will not be stable, we aim for a high estimation standard. It is well recognized that correctly estimating distributed lag models is a formidable econometric problem.[15] Generally, it is difficult to provide convincing evidence to a knowledgeable audience that *any* such model has been reliably estimated. Unless it has been carefully established that the correct lag length is known, the causality direction is established by testing, and structural changes, if any, are properly accounted for, any estimation of a distributed lag model must be considered doubtful. While several estimation procedures are available, their relative merits are not well known; no one procedure is recognized as superior. And the usual tests employed with time-series regressions often have to be used with considerable caution when distributed lags are involved.

A serious study involving as its mainstay shifting distributed lag model estimations must be a two-pronged affair. First, a thoughtfully laid-out *testing procedure* must be detailed with attention to estimation methods, sensitivity tests, and standards of evidence. Second, the entire results of that specific testing process must be readily accessible to the reader. Otherwise the quality of the evidence relative to the merits of the testing procedure cannot be determined by the knowledgeable reader, rightfully cautious when examining distributed lag model estimations. While these comments apply to any econometric effort, they are mandatory if a high econometric standard involving distributed lags is desired. Few distributed lag model estimations merit the label "final results." If in this book (especially

Chapters 3 and 4) it appears that we are beating a dead horse, then it is because econometrically dead horses have a nasty habit of coming to life after a study is in print. The following sections briefly discuss estimation problems, sensitivity analysis techniques, identifying structural change, and interpreting estimations of distributed lag models.

a. Estimation Problems

For many (most) economic models often we know how to specify the explanatory variables and from theory and/or other models know the expected signs of the coefficients. On occasion we can roughly approximate expected values of coefficients. Much of the econometric effort is ordinarily spent determining the particular form in which the variables best enter the model. However, where distributed lags are involved, we usually do not know (1) how many explanatory variables are required, i.e. the lag length, or (2) the approximate "shape" of the distribution of lag coefficients.

Typically, the correct lag length has to be determined by considerable econometric trial and error. We have to determine how many explanatory variables, i.e. lags, belong in the model as well as face the problem of correctly estimating their coefficients. What makes this a particularly vexing problem is that the conventional distributed lag estimating techniques are reliable if and only if the lag length is correctly specified *prior* to estimation. In general, estimations of distributed lag models are unreliable unless there is convincing evidence that the correct lag has already been determined. While this may seem like a chicken-and-egg situation, rigorous application of sensitivity tests in principle can determine if there is a correct lag. Ideally, we would like our estimation methods to be robust to lag length misspecification, i.e. not be sensitive to an incorrect specification of the lag length. The upshot is that there is no reason to have faith in any distributed lag estimation *unless* there is strong evidence suggesting that the correct lag has been determined.

In addition to the almost inevitable *econometric discovery* associated with correctly estimating distributed lag models, our study has the additional task of specifying the explanatory variable, money growth. Fortunately, we do not have a serious specification problem for the dependent variable. There is a premium on computationally convenient methods; the Almon method, despite its sensitivity to lag misspecification error, is especially useful as a trial horse technique.[16] Its especially attractive characteristic is that the degrees of freedom in estimation are independent of lag length specification. Once the lag pattern is restricted so that the coefficients are represented by a polynomial, usually of third or fourth degree, no more degrees of freedom are used up in estimating a 5- or 20-quarter distributed lag. (A third-degree Almon uses up 5 degrees of freedom.) No obvious penalty is extracted for experimenting with alternative lag lengths. This feature allows intensive sensitivity tests to be made with relatively small-sized samples; and were this feature not available, only a limited sensitivity analysis could be undertaken. In order not to be dependent on any one method, promising models will be reestimated with the Beynesian-based Shriller method.[17] This increasingly popular method does extract a degree of freedom for each lag period specified, is less sensitive to lag specification error, but is computationally awkward. We will also check with OLS, although its reliability as a distributed lag estimation procedure is uncertain.[18]

b. Sensitivity Analysis

Estimating and testing distributed lag models requires extensive use of standard sensitivity tests and also some special procedures. In this book, sensitivity analysis needs be carried out in two dimensions—identifying the correct lag structure for any given monetary aggregate and choosing among alternative money specifications. The latter procedure is usually referred to as *specification* analysis. Basically, for the standard procedures, subperiods are generated from a given size sample period. Each of these subperiods is then used to estimate the model; in turn, the estimated models are used to make dynamic out-of-sample forward simulations. In this manner, the model's sensitivity to sample selection is determined. The nonstandard procedures are called *straddle* tests and are designed to identify an optimum length lag once the approximate length has been determined. Since these sensitivity techniques are the major analytical tools used in this study, we discuss them briefly. (The straddle tests will be clarified with actual examples in Section 3.3.)

In using the 1956-1971 sample period and quarterly data, the standard sensitivity procedures can generate 30 sample subperiods, each of which provides the basis for post 1971 out-of-sample dynamic forward-simulation experiments. First, sample subperiods are generated by fixing the initial sample point at 1956 and successively extending the endpoint in yearly increments, beginning in 1962. In this fashion, 10 subperiods are generated—1956-1962, 1956-1963, 1956-1964, and so on. Second, the sample endpoint is fixed at 1971, and we work backward. Again 10 subperiods are generated—1965-1971, 1964-1971, and so on. Third, another set of 10 subperiods is generated, each 24 quarters long, in which both the initial and end sample points move forward successively each year. The respective intervals are 1956-1962, 1957-1963, and so on.

Note that the shortest of these sample subperiods has but 24 observations, below the usually accepted minimum of 25 for estimation methods, like the Almon, based on classical large sampling theory. (With a third-degree polynomial approximation, the Almon method uses 5 degrees of freedom, leaving but 19 available.) Estimations for these "short" sample periods will not be reliable, but it is useful when undertaking sensitivity analysis of distributed lag models to cast a broad net.

Now after these 30 subperiods have been selected and a particular monetary aggregate chosen, some lag length must be selected prior to estimation. One approach is to start with a fairly long lag, say 20 quarters, and if necessary, work backward toward shorter lags, expecting to see some evidence of the "true" lag structure, assuming one is to be found. To conserve scarce estimation resources, the overlapping sample sensitivity test is a good trial procedure. The lengthening sample tests can then be used selectively together with dynamic out-of-sample forward simulation.

Once careful use of these standard sensitivity tests has determined the approximately correct lag length (assuming that it is possible to find one) for some money specification, we can then use straddle test procedures to determine if there is an optimal lag length. For the first straddle test, the previously determined approximate lag length is straddled with models having both shorter and longer lag specifications. Using standard statistical tests and dynamic forward-simulation experiments, we then determine if there's an econometrically identifiable optimum lag. For the second straddle test, called a sideways straddle test, the initial lag lengths are progressively constrained to zero while the fixed lag length is shifted sideways; i.e. the lag distribution is shifted backward into time. In effect, we are testing where in the lag distribution a fixed length lag belongs.

We are not yet done, because any promising money specification should be disaggregated to see if its components are individually correctly specified. And if we obtain good results with quarterly data, semiannual growth data should also be used. Finally, promising models need be reestimated with other estimation techniques, and differences, if any, need to be reconciled. Perhaps another complete sensitivity analysis may be required with the alternative estimation method.

c. *Structural Change*

In estimating econometric models over fairly long sample periods, say several decades, it is commonly observed that they undergo structural change, occasionally for reasons that are hard to explain. In view of the special role attached to the constant term in our model, we expect a correctly specified monetarist inflation model to shift over time. It seems prudent, therefore, to consider the problems of identifying structural change in distributed lag models and how they may affect our study.

While our sample period is relatively long, about 60 quarters (mid or late 1950s to 1971), it is relatively short for purposes of estimating distributed lag models where a lag of several years and structural change are expected. Indeed, it is not too difficult to show that if structural changes do occur in the monetarist inflation models used in this study, they must occur no later than the early 1960s if we are to correctly estimate them. Also, if they do occur, it will be unusually difficult to identify them with any confidence.

When structural changes occur in distributed lag models, the usual circumstance is that they will be a three-dimensional affair, involving changes in lag length, in lag coefficients, and in the constant. In the special case where only the constant changes its value, the structural change is then identified as a structural *shift*, wherein the lag distribution simply shifts up or down. Unfortunately, there is no general testing procedure that correctly identifies how and when a structural change occurs in distributed lag models. This should not be surprising inasmuch as the conventional estimation methods are valid under the demanding assumption that the correct lag length is known beforehand and that it applies to the entire period used for estimation. As a practical matter, in estimating distributed lag models, sensitivity tests are used first to identify the correct lag length for a portion of the sample period for which it is thought that no structural change occurs. It is precisely because in the beginning the correct lag length and nature of the structural change, if any, are unknown that estimating distributed lags is so challenging. If it is assumed that no structural change occurred in the sample period and one, in fact, does occur, then the lag length will be incorrectly identified. This occurs with the M_1 monetarist inflation model, and the failure to test for structural change (i.e. stability tests) readily explains why the almost half-dozen or so previously reported results of estimating these models in the literature came up with different length lags. (See Section 3.3.)

If the lag is several years long, as seems likely for the monetarist inflation models we are studying, then a sample period of at least seven or eight years will be required to perform the full battery of sensitivity tests needed to test for stability. Since to support the thesis we require a model stable for a sample period ending in mid-1971, an acceptable model *must* be stable from at least the early 1960s onward. In order to generate post-1971/2 dynamic forward simulations required to test the thesis, a pre-1971 model with satisfactory stability characteristics must be available to test predominance of money growth after 1971/2. If a structural change occurs in the mid or late 1960s, then the required model will not be available for our forward-simulation experiments. We will not be able to test predominance, and the monetarist inflation thesis will be rejected.

Now, structural changes generally take place over several years as the change works its way through the lag structure. If the change takes place as late as the early 1960s, then after allowing three or four years for the change to occur, only four or five years are available to identify the "prechange" model. But four or five years (mid-1950s to, say, 1959) are hardly adequate for a thorough sensitivity analysis. Of course, if the structural change occurs prior to the early 1960s, the available prechange sample period will be too short for any estimation of the prechange model.

If structural change does occur, say in the early 1960s, conceptually we can work backward with the known stable model and use dummy variables on the constant term and the lag coefficients to econometrically identify the features of the structural change. These tests are best explained in Chapter 3 where not unexpectedly a structural change does occur and a significant portion of the econometric resources available to this study are devoted to identifying that change.

d. *Interpretation*

As a general rule of thumb, individual estimations of distributed lag models must be treated with considerable caution unless solid evidence has been garnered that the correct lag length has been identified, no unknown structural changes are involved, and the causality direction is supported. Usually the statistics reported are adjusted R^2 (standard error), F statistic, coefficients and t values of the individual distributed lags and their sum, and the constant term. Experience suggests that the statistical significance of the sum of coefficients (i.e. a sum at least twice its estimated standard error) need not imply anything about the significance of individual coefficients. For each of the lag coefficients to achieve significance in a fairly long lag, the t statistic value for the sum must often be at least 7 or 8; i.e. an estimated sum is 7 or 8 times greater than its standard error. In this book a *significant* distributed lag is one in which *all* the individual coefficients are individually significant, not merely their sum. Similarly, a *stable* distributed lag is one in which *all* the individual lag coefficients are stable. These standards of stability and significance in distributed lags are more rigorous than conventional usage.

A common occurrence with distributed lag model estimations is that once an appreciable lag has been specified, an apparently respectable-sized R^2 is obtained; however, many coefficients may not be significant, and varying the lag length may not affect the estimated R^2. The same is true for the sum of lag coefficients. Out-of-sample forward simulations often can be quite helpful in discriminating between alternative lag formulations. There are a good many examples in Chapters 3 and 4 that illustrate that the usual tests of statistical significance and discrimination seem to lose their "force" with respect to distributed lags. One useful clue is to watch the estimated constant term. Otherwise, respectable estimations with a large constant term are clearly misspecified. Manipulating the lag length on occasion finds its just reward in the size of the constant term!

2.4 Causality Direction

Much of the skepticism directed at the monetarist inflation thesis arises from the bold assertion of unidirectional causality running from money growth to inflation. If one is firmly skeptical about this assertion, then even strong results showing that unidirectional causality is possible (which have not been available before) may not be reassuring. To be sure, the issue cannot be resolved on theoretical grounds. What is needed is evidence. Fortunately, the causality issue is very much part and parcel of the econometric issue of whether monetarist inflation models are valid. Estimations of distributed lag models are econometrically valid if and only if the unidirectional causality is correctly specified.[19] Therefore, a *necessary* requirement for a serious econometric study involving distributed lags is causality testing. A sizable portion of the estimation resources available to this study are directed at this task.

The widely accepted definition of causality between any pair of time-series variables is due to C.W.J. Granger. Roughly expressed, it states that X "causes" Y if current values of Y can be more accurately predicted by past values of X compared to any other combination of values of X and Y.[20] The first practical procedure for testing Granger causality was developed by Christopher Sims and relies on careful use of distributed lag time-series regressions involving both past and future lags of X and Y[21].

The basic idea in a Sims/Granger test, as applied to our study, is that if causality is unidirectional, running form changes in money growth to changes in inflation, then in a time-series regression explaining inflation by past and future lags of money growth, the future lag coefficients should not be statistically significant. A variety of regressions are estimated, interchanging the positions of money growth and inflation. Since the test depends on the significance and size of future lag coefficients, the F test is carefully used to first ascertain that the regression estimations are statistically significant. Typically the data are pre-filtered, i.e. whitened, to ensure that serial correlation will not be present among the residuals after estimation and thus fulfill the F test requirements. Spectral density analysis of the residuals often is used to test for the presence of serial correlation. Also, sample homogeneity tests using the Chou test are appropriate. Finally, it should be emphasized that all the problems conventionally associated with estimating distributed lag time-series regressions may be present in any testing procedure that depends on distributed lags.

For a predetermined homogenous sample, four regressions are required: past and future lags of money growth on, i.e. explaining, inflation; the reverse regression; future lags of inflation on money growth; and the reverse regression. Functionally, they are expressed as follows:

$$\dot{P} = f(\text{past and future } \dot{M}) \tag{2.6}$$

$$\dot{M} = k(\text{past and future } \dot{P}) \tag{2.7}$$

$$\dot{P} = g(\text{future } \dot{M}) \tag{2.8}$$

$$\dot{M} = h(\text{future } \dot{P}) \tag{2.9}$$

Strong support for the null hypothesis—unidirectional causality running from changes in money growth to changes in inflation—requires significant regressions (F test) and that the future lag coefficients be significant (t test) in regressions (2.7) and (2.9) but not in (2.6) and (2.8). These are the strongest possible results.

We also look at the size and position of both significant and nonsignificant future lag coefficients. And the specification of the number of past and future lags may create some difficulties because ordinarily the regression will be misspecified as regards lag length.

A more detailed discussion accompanies an extended discussion of the actual test results in Section 3.7. The reader unfamiliar with this procedure will be rewarded by closely inspecting the full test results presented in the appendices to Chapter 3. The tests are by no means mechanical and require statistical judgment.

2.5 Predominance of Monetary Inflation

The monetarist inflation thesis does not claim that past money growth will always satisfactorily explain inflation. But it does suggest that as a general rule, money growth will continue to be the predominant determinant of inflation. The post-1971/2 period, beginning with the onset of wage/price controls, provides a good opportunity to test this proposition *provided* the thesis has been supported by an econometrically reliable model that adequately explains pre-1971 inflation. There is certainly no shortage of nonmonetary explanations for the inflation surge of the 1970s, e.g. the quadruple oil price hike. However, if the thesis is correct, the only lasting influence from these factors can be a permanent rise in the price level. They cannot be a continuing *source* of inflation.

The test for predominance is as follows. Suppose an econometrically reliable model based on Equation (2.5), our general monetarist inflation model, has been identified for the pre-1971 period; exogeneity has been confirmed by causality tests; the money-price elasticity is stable; and the distributed lag of money growth on inflation together with the trend term accounting for the nonmonetary factors provides a respectable explanation of inflation. Then, in these happy circumstances, an out-of-sample dynamic forward simulation is made beginning in mid-1971 using actual money growth figures. The forecast errors represent inflation not explained by money growth and the trend term.

Now, in looking at the forecast errors, predominance can be assessed in one of two ways: on a quarter-by-quarter basis or for the period as a whole. Somewhat arbitrarily, we cut off the simulation period in late 1975, two years after the oil price hike. In all, the simulation runs for 18 quarters, or 4½ years, from mid-1971 to late 1975, and includes the surge in inflation from 7 to 12 percent between late 1973 and late 1974. If on a quarter-by-quarter basis predicted inflation exceeds the forecast errors, then monetary inflation predominates (with due allowance for our trend term). That would be a strong result. To assess the entire period, we construct two price indices, both beginning mid-1971—one for actual inflation and another for predicted inflation. If by late 1975 the differences between the indices is less than the yearly increase in the price level generated on the average by money growth during the simulation period, then we can say that money growth predominated.

The two indices provide the basis for an important test originally proposed by Karnosky.[22] If they remain parallel, say beginning in late 1975, then we have good evidence that the unusual price effects during the simulation period simply raised the price level and were not a continuing *source* of inflation.

Note that we can say that the forecast errors represent nonmonetary inflation in the sense that *ordinarily* we recognize that output and velocity effects on the price level are captured by our constant, or trend, term. The test for predominance is a test of whether this formulation is satisfactory also for the 1971-1975 period. It is not a test of whether inflation is determined *only* by money growth. Our model does not say that. It is a test of whether the period from mid-1971 to late 1975 is fundamentally different from the period from mid-1950 to mid-1971.

In closing this chapter, it is worth noting that this test, like the model represented in Equation (2.5), gives useful evidence if the results are positive but only ambiguous evidence if they are not. For example, if the constant term shifts dramatically, implying structural change, then the test results may be unclear. There is a premium on the continued stability of this model throughout the simulation period. Stability can be assessed in terms of sensitivity tests and also whether the pre-1971 model gives good forecasts when the forward simulation is extended even further into 1976 and 1977. If that happens, the model used here will provide strong evidence supporting the thesis. Moreover, we will have an unusual macroeconomic model, one that survives a five-year forward simulation.

Notes

1. T. Mayer, "The Structure of Monetarism: I," *Kredit and Kapital* (April 1975): 209.

2. A.R. Nobay and H. Johnson, "Monetarism: A Historic-Theoretic Perspective," *Journal of Economic Literature* 15, no. 2 (June 1977): 470-85.

3. Nobay and Johnson, ibid., esp. pp. 476-80. The major approaches to the transmission problem are the rational expectations model, R.E. Lucas, Jr. (1972) and T. Sargent and N. Wallace (1976), and the general equilibrium models of K. Brunner and A. Meltzer (1972).

R.E. Lucas, Jr., "Expectations and the Neutrality of Money," *Journal of Economic Theory* (April 1972): 102-24; T.J. Sargent and N. Wallace, "Rational Expectations and the Theory of Economic Policy," *Journal of Monetary Economics* 2, no. 2 (April 1976): 169-83; K. Brunner and A. Meltzer, "Money, Debt and Economic Activity," *Journal of Political Economy* 80, no. 5 (September and October, 1972): 951-77.

4. D. Karnosky, "The Link between Money and Prices, 1971-76," *Review* of the Federal Reserve Bank of St. Louis, June 1976, pp. 17-23; L. Andersen and D. Karnosky, "The Appropriate Time Frame for Controlling Monetary Aggregates: The St. Louis Evidence," in *Controlling Monetary Aggregates II: The Implementation,* Conference Series No. 9 (Federal Reserve Bank of Boston, September 1972), pp. 147-77.

5. M. Keran, "Toward an Explanation of Simultaneous Inflation-Recession," *Business Review* of the Federal Reserve Bank of San Francisco, Spring 1975, pp. 18-30; R. Selden, "Inflation: Are We Winning the Fight?" *The Morgan Guaranty Survey*, October 1977, pp. 7-13; M. Levy, "Constraining Inflation: Causes, Complacencies and Evidence," *The Conference Board Record*, 12, no. 10, pp. 8-14. Unlike the other studies, Levy has serious doubts about the relationship because some of the earlier coefficients in his 15-quarter lag are negative.

6. E. Fiege and D. Pearce, "The Substitutability of Money and Near Monies: A Survey of the Time-Series Evidence," *Journal of Economic Literature* 15, no. 2 (June 1977): 439-69.

7. For a recent historical discussion on defining money see F. Pryor, "The Origins of Money," *Journal of Money, Credit and Banking* (August 1977): 391-409.

8. On the specification of the money-income relationship see M. Ham-

burgher, "The Lag Effect of Monetary Policy: A Survey of Recent Literature," in *Monetary Aggregates and Monetary Policy* (Federal Reserve Bank of New York, 1974), pp. 104-113.

9. Targets were officially posted in response to House Concurrent Resolution 133 in the spring of 1975. A useful history of FOMC operating ranges (both specified and actual) for M_1 and M_2 aggregates is found in Table 1, p. 3, of A. Burger and D. Mudd, "The FOMC in 1976: Progress against Inflation," *Review* of the Federal Reserve Bank of St. Louis, March 1977, pp. 2-17.

10. However, Richard Davis of the New York Federal Reserve suggests 6 months is a suitable time horizon for control. See R. Davis, "Implementing Open Market Policy with Monetary Aggregate Objectives," *Monetary Aggregates and Monetary Policy* (Federal Reserve Bank of New York, 1974), pp. 7-19.

11. See Carl F. Christ, "Judging the Performance of Econometric Models of the U.S. Economy," *International Economic Review* 16, no. 1 (February 1975): 54-74; and Gary Fromm and Lawrence Klein, "A Comparison of Eleven Econometric Models of the United States," *American Economic Review* (May 1973): 385-93.

12. Jürg Niehans, "How to Fill an Empty Shell," *American Economic Review* (May 1976): 177-83. A fourth reserve aggregate, reserves adjusted for changes in reserve requirements, would have been an important specification to have examined, but resource limitations precluded its investigation.

13. C. Sims, "Distributed Lags," in M. Intriligator (ed.), *Frontiers of Quantitative Economics*, vol. 2 (North Holland, 1974). Unadjusted figures were not available to this study.

14. The Federal Reserve could not control the money stock if it was purposefully committed to pegging government security prices. See M. Friedman and A. Schwartz, *A Monetary History of the United States* (Princeton University for NBER, 1963), pp. 13 and 623ff. If money growth is not exogenous relative to inflation, then the monetarist inflation model is not testable with conventional techniques.

15. A detailed discussion of the distributed lag estimation problem with reference to the literature is found in Sims, "Distributed Lags."

16. On the relative sensitivity of the Almon technique to lag misspecification see T. Cargill and R. Meyer, "Some Time and Frequency Domain Distributed Lag Estimators: A Comparative Monte Carlo Study," *Econometrica* 42, no. 6 (November 1974): 1031-44; and R. Shiller, "A Distributed Lag Estimator Derived from Smoothness Priors," *Econometrica* 41, no. 4 (July 1973): 775-88. The basic reference on the Almon method is S. Almon, "The Distributed Lag between Capital Appropriations and Expenditures," *Econometrica* 33 (1965): 178-96.

17. See Shiller, "A Distributed Lag Estimator," and R. Shiller, "Alternative Prior Representations of Smoothness for Distributed Lag Estimation," NBER *Working Paper No. 89*, NBER Computer Research Center, Cambridge, Massachusetts. Resource limitations precluded sensitivity analysis with this attractive method.

18. OLS has been given high marks by Cargill and Meyer, "Some Time and Frequency Domain Distributed Lag Estimators." The conventional opinion on the bias of OLS estimators in distributed lag models is found in J. Johnson, *Econometric Methods* (New York: McGraw-Hill, 1963), pp. 211-21. Almon, Shiller, and OLS were the only methods available to this study.

19. C. Sims, "Money, Income and Causality," *American Economic Review* 62, no. 4 (September 1972): 540-52.

20. C.W.J. Granger, "Investigating Causal Relations by Econometric Models and Cross Spectral Models," *Econometrica* 37 (July 1969): 424-38.

21. Sims, "Money, Income and Causality." For a related testing procedure using cross-correlation analysis see L.D. Haugh, "Checking and Independence of Two Covariance Stationary Time Series: A Univariate Residual Cross-Correlation Approach," *Journal of the American Statistical Association* (June 1976): 378-85.

22. Karnosky, "The Link between Money and Prices, 1971-76."

3 Testing the Monetarist Inflation Model with an M_1 Specification

3.1 Introduction and Summary

This chapter tests the first part of the monetarist inflation thesis with M_1, the most common definition of money, and finds unexpected strong econometric support for a correctly specified M_1 model. The correctly specified M_1 model has a 10-quarter uniformly distributed lag. Since 1956, this model explains almost 70 percent of the variability of inflation. The 11 weights or distributed lag coefficients (for the current and 10 past quarters) have identical values, implying that the price effects of the monetary impulse gradually extend over several years. The results of Sims/Granger tests strongly support unidirectional causality running from changes in M_1 growth to inflation.

As expected, the model shifts, but it does so only once during the past 20 years. In the early 1960s, the constant shifted downward by about 2.5 percentage points. In addition to unidirectional causality support and strong explanatory power, the money growth-inflation relationship is stable; the 1.4 estimated elasticity is stable throughout the entire sample period. When the model is forward-simulated, beginning in mid-1971 with the onset of controls, it underforecasts [mean absolute error (MAE)] by about 2 percent points until late 1975. However, for 1976 and 1977 it tracks rather nicely with an average forecast error of about 0.5 percentage point. An unusual feature of the sample period is that between 1963 and 1971 the R^2 rises to 0.8 and the residuals are both normally distributed and serially uncorrelated. The implication for this period is that stochastically, M_1 growth completely explains inflation provided provision is made for a growth trend or constant term.

This chapter is divided into seven parts. A preliminary sensitivity analysis in Section 3.2 suggests that 10 quarters is the approximately correct lag length specification for the 1960s. In Section 3.3, a thorough sensitivity analysis is vigorously applied to the M_1 model and unambiguously establishes that 10 quarters is the correct lag specification for the 1963-1971 period. Then in Section 3.4 a closer look at the individual lag coefficients with alternative estimation procedures finds that they have the simplest distribution—a uniform one. Tests of the residuals find that they are normally distributed and serially uncorrelated.

In Section 3.5, a post-1971/2 stability testing of the M_1 model is made with sensitivity tests and dynamic forward simulation. Section 3.6 identifies the structural change in the early 1960s previously found in preliminary sensitivity analysis as a structural shift. The last section of this chapter applies the Sims/Granger procedure for testing whether causality runs unidirectionally as hypothesized from changes in M_1 growth to changes in inflation. A selective review of the specific test results of the analyses conducted in this chapter is discussed below.

A thorough sensitivity analysis firmly supports that 10 quarters is the correct lag specification from mid-1963 through the end of the sample period, mid-1971. Overlapping, lengthening sample, straddle, and sideways straddle sensitivity tests each clearly support 10 quarters as the correct lag specification without initial lag constraints. Furthermore, when M_1 is disaggregated into its components, demand deposits and currency, sensitivity analyses with these components confirms that the M_1 model has been correctly specified. A 10-quarter-lag demand deposit model is statistically identical to the M_1 model. The currency model is correctly specified at 9 quarters and has a larger elasticity, about 2. A straddle sensitivity test using semiannual data confirms that the lag is correctly specified at 2½ years. For the 1963-1971 sample period, the M_1 model explains about 80 percent of the variance in inflation using quarterly data and 90 percent using semiannual data.

Reestimating the M_1 model with the preferred Shiller technique yields statistically identical regression statistics but implies that the "true" population lag coefficients are uniformly distributed rather than having an inverted saucer shape as suggested by the Almon method.

Lengthening and overlapping sample sensitivity tests suggest that the previously identified 10-quarter-lag M_1 model remains stable after 1971/2. This is an important finding since this period is commonly thought to include unusual nonmonetary price effects. A dynamic out-of-sample forward simulation beginning in 1971/2 finds that the M_1 model satisfactorily tracks inflation beginning in late 1975, further confirming the stability assessment made with sensitivity tests.

Reversing direction, structural change tests find strong evidence that in the early 1960s the model shifted downward by about 2.5 percentage points for reasons that are not fully clear. Some simulation tests suggested that the phasing-in of vault cash in fulfillment of reserve obligations is partially responsible in that it makes for a more orderly structural transition, but is not a causal determinant. The M_1 model, then, is stable over more than two decades, except for a downward shift in the early 1960s. However, the M_1-price elasticity, 1.4, is demonstrably stable throughout the entire period.

Sims procedure for testing Granger causality was applied to four sample periods of known but differing characteristics: 1963-1971, 1956-1971, 1963-1976, and the entire sample period 1956-1976. The results strongly support the null hypothesis of unidirectional causality running from changes in money growth to changes in inflation. These test results are important on two counts. First, they fulfill the requirements that the unidirectional causality assumption in distributed lag estimations should be tested. Second, by showing that unidirectional causality is possible between money growth and inflation, they provide some hard evidence on whether a single-equation monetarist inflation model is a sensible format.

3.2 Approximating the Correct Lag Specification

Since *some* initial lag must be specified before the M_1 model can be estimated, a 20-quarter lag is arbitrarily selected. The 20-quarter-lag M_1 model has appeared twice in the literature, but unaccompanied by the results of any sensitivity analysis.[1] Simply dividing the sample period into two contrasting subperiods (moderate 2 percent inflation until 1965 and 4 percent thereafter) and comparing the estimations for these subperiods with that for the entire period easily identifies that a 20-quarter-lag M_1 model is misspecified. The estimation for the first subperiod is not statistically significant while that for the second has no significant lag coefficients. Note that the estimation for the entire period is significant (all coefficients except that of the current period are significant) with a proportional M_1-price elasticity; half the variance is explained. These results, however, are unreliable; no confidence is warranted in a model whose estimations for each of two reasonably chosen subperiods are not statistically significant.[2] Indeed, these three estimations nicely illustrate the requirement that distributed lag model estimations should always be accompanied by the results of at least *some* supporting sensitivity analysis.

When preliminary sensitivity testing gives poor or conflicting results, often it is useful to undertake a more detailed testing, especially with the overlapping sample sensitivity procedure. This may show that the model is suitable for only part of the sample period, implying that perhaps a structural change took place and/or suggesting modifications of the originally specified model. To make this test, the sample period is divided into 10 overlapping subperiods, each six years long. The first begins in 1956 and ends in 1962; the second begins and ends one year later, 1957-1963; and so on. These 24-quarter subperiods are certainly on the short side since after estimation only 19 degrees of freedom are left. Inasmuch as the Almon method is based on classical statistical decision procedures, estimations with less than 25 degrees of freedom are of questionable reliability. With that caveat the estimations are useful for preliminary analysis. Note that when an initial date is given for a sample period, say 1956, that means that 1956/1 is the first available quarter for which data will be available to estimate the entire distributed lag. A sample period beginning in 1956 uses money growth data beginning 10 quarters earlier, 1953/3, for a 10-quarter lag.

The estimations for the 10 overlapping sample periods convincingly suggest that the 20-quarter-lag M_1 model is misspecified. Only the estimations for the first and last four subperiods are statistically significant; an appreciable number of significant coefficients appear in but two adjoining subperiods, 1962-1968 and 1963-1969. They share five lags in common—0, 1, 2, 3, and 10—suggesting that a shorter lag specification, say 10 quarters, may be worth examining, at least from the early 1960s onward. The overlapping sample estimations for the 20-quarter-lag M_1 model are presented in Table 3A-1.

The overlapping sample sensitivity test was repeated but with a 10-quarter-lag specification. For each of the last three subperiods, spanning the interval from 1963/2 to 1971/2, the estimations are statistically significant, as are the distributed lags. For the purpose of this study, a distributed lag is said to be statistically significant only when the coefficient of *each* lag period is significant (t statistic test), not merely the sum of coefficients. (Inspection of Table 3A-1 readily reveals that significance of the sum alone does not imply that a distributed lag has any significant coefficients.) Each of the three estimations explains about 70 percent of the variance in inflation and yields a statistically nonproportional M_1-price elasticity (sum of lag coefficients) estimate of about 1.5. The elasticity is nonproportional because the lower bound of its 95 percent confidence interval is greater than 1. Note that for this study the reported R^2 statistic is always adjusted for degrees of freedom. Together the three estimations provide preliminary evidence that the 10-quarter-lag specification is appropriate for the 1963-1971 period. They are presented in the top half of Table 3-1; complete tabulations of the 10 estimations used in the overlapping sample sensitivity test appear in Table 3A-2. These relatively strong findings with the overlapping sample sensitivity test suggest that a more detailed sensitivity analysis of the M_1 model with a 10-quarter-lag specification is warranted.

3.3 Sensitivity Analysis of the 10-Quarter Lag M_1 Model, 1963-1971

To further examine whether the M_1 model is correctly specified with a 10-quarter lag for the 1963-1971 sample period, a variety of additional sensitivity tests were made. (The foregoing overlapping sample sensitivity tests suggest 1963/2 as an initial sample point. A more detailed analysis is made in Section 3.6.) These include lengthening sample, straddle, sideways straddle, straddle with semiannual rather than quarterly growth figures, and disaggregation tests.

Table 3-1
Overlapping and Lengthening Sample Sensitivity Tests, 10-Quarter-Lag M_1 Model, 1963-1971

Sample Period	Sum of Coefficients (t Values)	R^2/Standard Error	Durbin-Watson Statistic	Lag Periods with Significant Coefficients	1971/3-1976/2 Simulation Statistics RMSE	MAE	Constant Term (t Value)
Overlapping Sample Estimations							
1963/2-1969/2	1.33 (6.68)	.68/.85	2.63	All	–		−2.40 (−3.11)
1964/2-1970/2	1.47 (7.59)	.70/.84	2.74	All	–		−2.96 (−3.32)
1965/2-1971/2	1.63 (7.20)	.68/.79	2.43	All	–		−3.78 (−3.38)
Lengthening Sample Estimations							
1963/2-1968/2	1.39 (5.41)	.62/.87	2.65	0-4,8-10	2.91	2.30	−2.64 (−2.64)
1963/2-1969/2	1.33 (6.68)	.68/.85	2.63	All	2.88	2.26	−2.40 (−3.11)
1963/2-1970/2	1.42 (9.32)	.76/.80	2.64	All	2.70	2.17	−2.65 (−3.99)
1963/2-1971/2	1.42 (10.46)	.78/.81	2.58	All	2.72	2.19	−2.67 (−4.29)

a. Lenthening Sample Test

The lengthening sample test requires generating a series of sample subperiods each beginning with the same initial sample date, 1963/2, but with progressively later sample endpoints. The endpoint of the first subperiod, 1968/2, allows but 15 degrees of freedom. Successive subperiods end in the second quarters of 1969, 1970, and 1971. The estimations of the four sample subperiods provide preliminary evidence that the 10-quarter-lag M_1 model is stable; they are presented in the bottom portion of Table 3-1. As the sample periods lengthen, the R^2 improves from 0.6 to 0.8 (standard errors decline to 0.8). The estimated M_1-price elasticity (sum of coefficients) is about 1.4 (statistically elastic, i.e. greater than 1), the distributed lag is significant, and the constant term is significant with a value of about −2.6. The statistics from the 1971/3–1976/2 out-of-sample forward simulations with each of the four estimated M_1 models (using actual M_1 growth values) are also reported in Table 3-1. The 1976/2 cutoff date for forward simulation was chosen simply because the estimations in this study were largely completed in the fall of 1976. As the sample period lengthens, there is some improvement in the forward-simulation statistics—root mean square error (RMSE) and mean absolute error (MAE). However, the simulation statistics are fairly similar; inflation is underforecast by about 2 percentage points.

b. Straddle Test

To test whether the M_1 model is optimized with a 10-quarter-lag specification for the 1963-1971 sample period, a *straddle* sensitivity test is made with both shorter and longer lag specifications. The model is reestimated with lags of 8, 9, 11, and 12 quarters in length for the 1963-1971 sample period. The estimations and forward simulations are presented in the top portion of Table 3-2. At 10 quarters, the standard error is minimized; for 8 quarters it is 1.03, then drops to 0.81 at 10 quarters and increases to 0.88 for 12 quarters. All the estimated lag coefficients are significant for the models with 8-, 9-, and 10-quarter lags, but when an eleventh lag is introduced, its estimated coefficient becomes nonsignificant. Adding a twelfth lag introduces yet another nonsignificant coefficient, while the eleventh lag coefficient remains nonsignificant. Note that the estimated sum of lag coefficients is invariant at 1.4 (statistically elastic) for a wide range of lag length specifications, 9 to 12 quarters. Looking at the post-1971/2 out-of-sample forward simulations in Table 3-2, we find that the RMSE and MAE are minimized at 10 quarters, but the decline in performance on either side is less than 10 percent. This straddle test, then, gives strong evidence that 10 quarters is the correct lag specification in an M_1 model for the 1963/2-1971/2 sample period.

c. Sideways Straddle Test

To test whether initial lag period coefficient constraints are required, a sideways straddle sensitivity test is made, arbitrarily imposing progressively lengthening initial lag point constraints, while retaining the fixed 10-quarter-lag length specification.[3] Sequentially, the lag includes past quarters 1-11, 2-12, 3-13, and so on. When the lag is shifted one quarter in this manner, i.e. the current quarter's lag is constrained to zero, there is a small increase in the standard error, but the distributed lag coefficients begin to lose significance with further sideways shifting. By the time the lag is shifted sideways three quarters (periods 3-13) the standard error increases by one-third; several coefficients and the constant term lose significance; the sum of coefficients statistically is now 1. This test suggests that the M_1 model is correctly specified at 10 quarters without any initial lag constraints. Further details are presented in Table 3A-3.

Table 3-2
Straddle Sensitivity Tests of the 2½-Year Lag M_1 Model, Quarterly and Semiannual Data, 1963-1971

Number of Lags	*Sum of Coefficients (t Value)*	*R^2/Standard Error*	*Lag Periods with Significant Coefficients*	*Constant Term (t Value)*	*1971/3-1976/2 Simulation Statistics*	
					RMSE	*MAE*
8 Quarters	1.24 (7.48)	0.63/1.03	0-8	−1.98 (−2.57)	3.05	2.47
9 Quarters	1.39 (9.80)	0.75/.85	0-9	−2.63 (−4.01)	2.74	2.28
10 Quarters	1.42 (10.46)	0.78/.81	0-10	−2.67 (−4.29)	2.72	2.19
11 Quarters	1.40 (9.41)	0.73/.89	0-10	−2.59 (−3.78)	2.72	2.17
12 Quarters	1.41 (9.48)	0.73/.88	0-10	−2.71 (−3.91)	2.82	2.24
4 Half-years	1.24 (9.24)	0.85/.60	0-4	−1.93 (−3.15)		
5 Half-years	1.27 (10.87)	0.88/.52	0-5	−1.95 (−3.65)		
6 Half-years	1.31 (10.61)	0.88/.53	0-5	−2.22 (−3.74)		

d. Straddle Test with Semiannual Data

It is also important to determine whether the 2½-year-lag M_1 model is correctly specified for M_1 growth and inflation figures computed over a longer time horizon. Accordingly, straddle sensitivity tests for the 1963-1971 sample period were made about a 5 semiannual lag M_1 model. For the 2½-year-lag specification, R^2 is 0.9 and the standard error is 0.5. Some of the additional explanation follows from a reduction in data variability as the time dimension is extended. The individual coefficients for each of the 5 semiannual lags are statistically identical (their confidence intervals overlap one another). Their sum, 1.3, is statistically identical to the 1.4 value obtained using quarterly lags, again implying that the M_1-price relationship is statistically nonproportional for the 1963-1971 period. When the sixth semiannual lag is added, it becomes nonsignificant, but not the previous ones. A 4 semiannual lag specification has a significantly larger standard error. Summary results are presented in the bottom portion of Table 3-2; the complete estimations appear in Table 3A-4.

e. Disaggregating M_1

Our confidence in the 10-quarter-lag specification for the M_1 model will be substantially reinforced if that specification also applies to the major component of M_1, demand deposits, and approximately to the minor component, currency.[4] A straddle test finds that the demand deposit monetarist inflation model is correctly specified at 10 quarters and statistically is identical to the M_1 model. The demand deposit-price elasticity is 1.3 for lag lengths of 10, 11, and 12 quarters. The standard error is minimized at 10 quarters, 0.80. For 11 quarters it is 0.89. Also, the *t* value of the elasticity, 10.73, suggests that the M_1-price elasticity is nonproportional. The M_1 model can thus be referred to as a demand deposit monetarist inflation model. The currency model is correctly specified (straddle test) at 9 quarters; its elasticity is 2.1, and R^2 is 0.6. Out-of-sample forward simulations with M_1 are slightly superior to those of the demand deposit model, and also are significantly superior to those from the demand deposit model combined with these from currency model.

3.4 A Closer Look at the 10-Quarter-Lag M_1 Model

The previous sensitivity tests conducted with the Almon estimation method—overlapping sample, lengthening sample, straddle, and disaggregation—suggest that for an M_1 monetarist inflation model, 10 quarters is the correct lag specification for the 1963/2-1971/2 sample period. We now examine the individual estimated lag coefficients, reestimate the model with alternative estimation methods, and test the estimation residuals.

a. The Distribution of Almon Lag Coefficients

On the whole, the 11 individually significant Almon distributed lag coefficients (current and 10 past periods) range in value from 0.09 (sixth period) to 0.20 (tenth period). Their distribution resembles a flat inverted saucer, a rather peculiar shape for any distributed lag. The lag coefficients have a mean value of 0.13, i.e. their estimated sum of coefficients, 1.42, divided by the number of periods, 11. Excluding the two lag coefficients at each end of the distribution (periods 0-1 and 9-10), the remaining seven coefficients are statistically identical; their respective 95 percent confidence intervals overlap one another. Statistically, then, the distribution is a uniform one with upward loadings on each tail; the tenth period has the largest loading with a value of 0.20. Note that the last lag of the 5 semiannual lag M_1 model also has a large loading (see Table 3A-4). Ordinarily, such a relatively large loading at the tail end of a distribution would imply that additional lag periods were required; however, a battery of sensitivity tests have previously suggested that the M_1 model is correctly specified at 10 quarters. The complete estimation of the model with the individual lag coefficients is presented in Table 3A-5.

It is useful to note what happens if the constant term is constrained to zero. The standard error increases from 0.81 to 1.01 and changes occur in the distributed lag characteristics. The elasticity drops from 1.42 to 0.85 with one-third of the weights concentrated in the ninth and tenth period lag coefficients. Also, the current lag coefficient becomes nonsignificant. All in all, we have a good example of the sensitivity of the Almon procedure to misspecification of initial lag constraints.

b. The Distribution of Shiller Lag Coefficients

The well-recognized problem of correctly estimating time-series regressions involving distributed lags requires that promising estimates be compared with those obtained from other accepted estimation methods. The estimation of the 10-quarter-lag M_1 model with the increasingly popular Shiller method is presented in Table 3A-5.

The Shiller method uses up 13 degrees of freedom in estimating a 10-quarter distributed lag, effectively precluding its use in the small-sample sensitivity analysis made in this chapter. The Shiller estimated sum of coefficients and standard error are statistically identical to the Almon estimates. However, there are some suggestive differences between the two distributions of lag coefficients. The distribution of the Shiller lag coefficients also resembles an inverted saucer, but the coefficients are symmetrically distributed about the fifth period's lag value of 0.10 and monitonically increase to values of 0.16 at either tail, avoiding the large loading characteristic of the Almon lag coefficient distribution. More significantly, all the Shiller lag coefficients *do* fall within the sample mean lag coefficient's 95 percent confidence interval bounds, 0.13 ± 0.034.

The Shiller coefficients, unlike the Almon coefficients, are statistically identical about their sample mean value of 0.13. This observation raises the interesting question, to be discussed below in Section 3.4d, of whether the population coefficients of the 10-quarter-lag M_1 model are uniformly sized. Recall that the Almon coefficients of the 5 semiannual lag M_1 model were also statistically identical to one another (see Table 3A-4).

c. An OLS Estimation

The 10-quarter-lag M_1 model was also estimated for the 33-quarter (1963/2-1971/2) sample period with OLS.[5] The estimates for the constant term and the sum of coefficients, −2.59 and 1.38, respectively, are statistically identical with those previously obtained with the Almon and Shiller methods. However, only 4 of the 11 lag coefficients, periods 0, 2, 7, and 10, are statistically significant. The conventional wisdom maintains that OLS estimations of distributed lag models are unreliable; however, the Cargill and Meyer Monte Carlo simulation of OLS, Almon, and Hannon procedures gave OLS high marks. Since an OLS estimation leaves only 20 degrees of freedom available, an assessment of the OLS distributed lag coefficients is difficult.

d. Are the Weights Uniform?

To inquire whether the lag coefficients are uniformly sized, a new model is specified. The uniformly weighted 10-quarter-lag M_1 model is specified as follows (for the 1963/2-1971/2 sample period):

$$p_t = -2.67 + \sum_{i=0}^{10} 0.13 m_{1_{t-i}} + u \qquad (3.1)$$

where p, m, and u have their previous meaning and each quarter's M_1 growth is weighted by the constant valued lag coefficient, 0.13. The null hypothesis is that the Almon and Shiller estimations are not statistically different from the uniformly weighted 10-quarter-lag model above. The selected testing statistics are the standard error (for the sample period) and the RMSE and MAE (for the post-1971/2 out-of-sample forward simulations). The sample means, are, of course, identical. For the uniformly weighted model, the standard error is obtained from a forward simulation beginning 1963/2 and ending 1971/2 since its parameters, —2.67 for the constant and 0.13 for the uniform lag weights, have already been predetermined.

A cursory inspection of the testing statistics for the Almon, Shiller, and uniformly weighted lag distributions suggests that a formal statistical design test procedure [e.g. using chi-square statistic to test for differences in sample standard errors (SE)] is unnecessary. The three sets of test statistics are nearly identical. Their values are as follows:

	Uniform Weighted Lag	*Almon*	*Shiller*
SE (1963-1971)	0.80	0.81	0.81
RMSE (1971-1976)	2.62	2.72	2.70
MAE (1971-1976)	2.18	2.19	2.18

These statistics suggest that the M_1 model is correctly specified with a uniformly weighted 10-quarter lag.

Several implications follow.

(1) For convenient forecasting, the sum of the current and 10 past values of M_1 growth rates, multiplied by 0.13 and added to the constant −2.67, yields the current quarter's inflation forecast. Alternatively, take the average of the current and 10 past M_1 growth rates, multiply by 1.42 and add the constant, −2.67. Ordinarily, results with this method will be nearly identical to forecasts with the Almon or Shiller lag weights simply because the M_1 growth rates are averaged over a 10-quarter period.

(2) Given the acknowledged difficulties in correctly estimating distributed lag models, finding that the correctly specified M_1 model has the simplest possible lag distribution with a well-defined optimum lag length suggests that the distribution has been indeed correctly identified at least for the 1963-1971 sample period. Econometrically, it is unlikely that, with a curvilinear distribution, sensitivity analysis would so robustly identify the correct lag, given the relatively short sample period of 33 quarters. Since distributed lag procedures typically do not give identical estimation results, we would expect that if the true lag were uniform, the differences would be perhaps only modest. This turns out to be the case. With a curvilinear lag distribution, considerably more energies would need be expended to select the "appropriate" estimation. With a uniform lag, the M_1 model has the not inconsiderable advantage of being "estimation-independent."

(3) With a robust uniformly distributed lag, structural change will likely involve parallel shifts of the entire distribution, i.e. a change only in the constant term, rather than in lag length or coefficients.

(4) If the population 10-quarter-lag M_1 model does have uniform weights as our analysis suggests, then some comparative but tentative evaluations can be made about the relative reliability of the Shiller and Almon methods. The Almon method had some difficulty in correctly distributing the lag weights; in particular, it suggested an implausible tail-end loading. To its credit, it used up only 5 degrees of freedom in estimation. The Shiller method comes out better in distributing lag coefficient weights, but requires more than twice as many degrees of freedom, an important limitation precluding sensitivity analysis of small samples. With generous-sized samples, the Shiller would deserve first consideration. Resource limitations prevented a parallel sensitivity analysis with the Shiller method. A comparative study of the abilities of various methods at sensitivity analysis involving a known uniformly distributed lag would be an informative one.

e. Distribution of Estimation Residuals

The stochastic form of the general monetarist inflation model, in common with with most econometric modeling, assumes that the estimation residuals are normally distributed. It is always in order to test whether this assumption is supported and to look for indications of excluded variables. Also since careful attention will be paid to the post-1971 out-of-sample forward simulation for testing of money growth predominance, the residuals preceding the onset of the simulation period should be carefully inspected.

A chi-square goodness-of-fit test easily supports the null hypothesis that the residuals are normally distributed, but the same point can be made more simply. The 1963/2-1971/2 sample period has 33 quarters. If the residuals are normally distributed, 68 percent (22 quarters) would be expected to fall within the interval bounded by ± 1 standard error, 0.81 percentage point, and 95 percent (32 quarters) within ± 2 standard errors, 1.62 percentage points. The actual count is 23, equally distributed about the residual mean (equal to zero), and 33, respectively. The Almon residuals, actual and estimated inflation figures for the sample period, are presented in Table 3A-6.

Although the Durbin-Watson statistic is not a completely satisfactory one for testing the presence of autocorrelated disturbances in distributed lag estimations (even when the data are expressed in growth rates), the D-W values in the bottom half of Table 3-1 do suggest that no additional variables are required in the 10-quarter-lag M_1 monetarist inflation model for the 1963/2-1971/2 period.

The residuals toward the latter portion of the sample period provide additional evidence that they are well behaved and suggest that the immediate post-1971/2 out-of-sample forward-simulation forecasts warrant close attention. For each of the last three years of the sample period, the residuals average out to zero. Also, the quarter immediately preceding the onset of wage/price controls, 1971/2, has a zero estimation residual. Thus, for an eight-year period, the 10-quarter-lag M_1 model explains about 80 percent of the variance in inflation, and its residuals imply that there are no excluded variables. Stochastically, for this period inflation is completely explained. The model is tracking inflation with commendable accuracy considering that price effects from the interactions of the monetary impulse with the real sector of the economy are not explicitly shown.

3.5 A Post-1971 Stability Testing of the 10-Quarter-Lag M_1 Model

A complete stability test of the M_1 model for the post-1971/2 period requires first dividing actual post-1971/2 inflation into both ordinary and extraordinary nonmonetary components and then determining whether the M_1 model satisfactorily explains ordinary inflation. Since the inflation component explained by the monetary impulse alone for this period is not yet known to us, our stability tests must be regarded as *formally* incomplete, even though they do suggest continued stability.

Two types of post-1971 stability assessment are made. The first uses two standard sensitivity procedures previously employed in this study, overlapping sample and lengthening sample tests. The Almon method is used solely for computational convenience. The second assessment examines the 8-quarter 1976-1977 tracking performance of the 10-quarter uniform lag M_1 model to determine if it "survives" the 1971-1975 unusual nonmonetary price effects.

a. Sensitivity Tests: Lengthening and Overlapping Samples

For the *lengthening* sample sensitivity test, the sample period (beginning in 1963/2) is progressively extended in yearly increments through 1976. We can thus observe the model's characteristics as the original eight-year sample period (of known stability) is gradually extended into a 13-year sample period involving unusual nonmonetary inflation. The estimation and forward-simulation statistics are presented in the top half of Table 3-3; they support the continued stability of the M_1 model. With but one exception, the estimated M_1-price elasticities statistically are not different from 1.4. Generally, the distributed lag structures retain significance, although in the last four estimations the current quarter's lag coefficient loses significance. The standard errors double in size from about 0.8 to 1.7, reflecting the surge of unusual nonmonetary inflation (R^2 declines from 0.8 to about 0.6). However, the increase in standard error takes place with the subperiod ending in 1975/2, suggesting that no additional unusual nonmonetary disturbances were introduced in the following year. Not unexpectedly, the forward simulations decline in forecasting ability, especially when 1973 is included in the sample.

For the *overlapping* sample sensitivity test, five sample subperiods were generated, each 24 quarters long. The first begins in 1966/2 and ends in 1972/2, covering five years of known stability and one year of unusual nonmonetary price effects. The initial and end sample points are progressively extended until the last sample period, 1970/2 and 1976/2, including one year of known stability. These estimations make strenuous demands on the model and the Almon estimation technique; only 19 degrees of freedom are available, well below the acceptable minimum for correctly specified models and robust estimation procedures. The estimation statistics are presented in bottom half of Table 3-3. The M_1-price elasticity estimates range from 1.4 to 2.0; one regression is not significant. Lag period coefficients 3 to 10 retain significance. Not unexpectedly, the R^2's decline sharply as the sample

Table 3-3
Lengthening and Overlapping Sample Sensitivity Tests, 10-Quarter-Lag M_1 Model, 1963-1976

Sample Period	*Sum of Coefficients (t Value)*	*R^2/Standard Error*	*Durbin-Watson Statistic*	*Lag Periods with Significant Coefficients*	*Constant Term (t Value)*	*1971/3-1976/2 Simulation Statistics RMSE*	*MAE*
			Lengthening Sample Estimations				
1963/2-1971/2	1.42 (10.46)	.78/.81	2.58	All	−2.67 (−4.29)	2.72	2.19
1963/2-1972/2	1.32 (8.77)	.68/.93	2.44	All	−2.27 (−3.25)	2.96	2.35
1963/2-1973/2	1.15 (8.85)	.66/.98	2.04	1-10	−1.58 (−2.49)	3.50	4.39
1963/2-1974/2	1.40 (8.56)	.64/1.35	1.09[b]	1-9	−2.47 (−2.98)	2.96	2.48
1963/2-1975/2	1.53 (7.86)	.63/1.66	0.89[b]	2-10	−2.83 (−2.81)	1.29	1.15
1963/2-1976/2	1.55 (8.12)	.63/1.63		2-10		–	–
			Overlapping Sample Estimations				
1966/2-1972/2	1.37 (4.12)	.36/1.02	2.30	All	−2.54 (−1.50)		
1967/2-1973/2[a]	0.86 (2.68)	.23/1.08	1.86	2-5, 9-10	.13 (.07)		
1968/2-1974/2	1.44 (2.72)	.29/1.66	0.84[b]	3-10	−2.78 (−.89)		
1969/2-1975/2	1.96 (2.91)	.38/2.09	0.73[b]	4-10	−5.58 (−1.39)		
1970/2-1976/2	1.73 (3.18)	.50/1.93	1.29[b]	3-10	−3.87 (−1.21)		

[a]*F* test denotes this estimation is not significant.
[b]Serially correlated residuals.

period is extended to include years with unusual nonmonetary price effects. Perhaps the most interesting estimation is that for 1970/2 to 1976/2, including one sample year completely free of unusual nonmonetary price effects; R^2 is 0.5, coefficients 3 to 10 are significant, and the elasticity is 1.7. Even in this short sample period dominated by unusual nonmonetary price effects, the underlying M_1 monetarist inflation model finds significant statistical support.

b. Post-1975 Forecasting Performance

Our second procedure for assessing the post-1971/2 stability characteristics of the 10-quarter-lag M_1 model examines whether the inflation forecasts come back on track when the simulation is further extended to 1976 and 1977. (Since we are going to press in early 1978, the last quarter for which it is possible to extend the simulation with known M_1 growth rates is 1977/4.) Presumably by late 1975 the unusual nonmonetary price effects that caused the forward simulation to underforecast inflation by about 2 percentage points between mid-1971 and 1975 had been accommodated into the general price structure. Although few models survive a five- and six-year out-of-sample forward simulation, for our purposes this is an appropriate stability test procedure. The findings are presented in Table 3-4.

For an out-of-sample forward simulation beginning 19 quarters after the sample period used to estimate the model, these are creditable forecasts, considering the simplicity of the model. The MAE is only 0.7 percentage point, less than 1 standard error. The only blooper in the lot, lying outside 2 standard errors (1.6), is the 2.3 percentage point underforecast in 1977/2. Excluding that quarter, inflation is underforecast by 0.5 percentage point on the average. An attractive feature of the forecast errors is that while they appear to decay in the middle of the period, they come back on track in the last two quarters.

These forecast errors indirectly shed some light on the importance of recent changes in the payments mechanism. There is little doubt that recent

Table 3-4
Inflation Forecasts with the M_1 Model, 1976-1977

Period	*(1)* *Actual Inflation*	*(2)* *Forecast Inflation*	*(1) – (2)* *Forecast Error*
1976/1	4.0%	3.9%	0.1%
/2	4.8	4.2	0.6
/3	4.5	4.1	0.4
/4	5.3	4.2	1.1
1977/1	5.2	4.0	1.2
/2	6.9	4.6	2.3
/3	4.8	5.2	–0.4
/4	6.2	6.0	0.2
Average	5.2	4.5	0.7

Note: Forecasts made from out-of-sample forward simulation with 10-quarter uniformly weighted lag M_1 model beginning 1971/3.

changes have occurred in the payments mechanism over the past several years. Indeed, they have been cited (perhaps incorrectly) as partially responsible for an apparent shift in the heretofore stable demand-for-money equation.[6] However, the forecasts suggest that any changes resulting in an economizing of cash balances to date have only had a modest effect on the forecasting prowess of the M_1 model. The first six quarters' forecast errors do suggest a tendency to underforecast, but the errors for the past half-year are nearly zero. More time is needed to determine whether the M_1 model requires an upward adjustment to account for payments mechanism changes.

3.6 Testing for Pre-1963 Structural Change

Previously reported overlapping sample sensitivity tests implied that a structural change occurred in the early 1960s. (See Table 3A-2 where overlapping sample estimations are not significant for the 1956-1965 period.) That change is now more carefully documented and is identified as a downward shift of about 2.5 percentage points. However, not unexpectedly, the cause of that shift remains unclear and warrants further study. Except for this structural shift, the 10-quarter lag M_1 model is stable from 1956 onward, explaining about 70 percent of the variability in inflation. Especially interesting is that the estimated 1.4 M_1-price elasticity remains *stable* for the entire post-1956 period.

a. Backward Lengthening Sample Sensitivity Test

A backward lengthening sample sensitivity test documents that a structural change occurred in the early 1960s. Retaining the 1971/2 endpoint, the initial sample point is progressively moved back in yearly increments. A one-year backward extension (to 1962/2) significantly changes the previously robust sum of coefficients and constant term to 1.1 (statistically 1) and −1.1, respectively. The constant term becomes statistically nonsignificant with an additional backward extension to 1961/2. With yet further yearly backward extensions to 1956/2, the same pattern holds: significant distributed lag coefficients (except for current period), proportional sum of lag coefficients, and a nonsignificant constant (statistically zero). By 1957, the standard error has increased from 0.81 to 1.12. Complete backward lengthening sample estimations of the 10-quarter-lag M_1 model in annual increments are presented in Table 3A-7.

b. Structural Change Tests

Structural changes are unusually difficult to correctly identify in distributed lag models, even when the model is correctly specified prior to the change, and usually they require extensive sensitivity analysis. Ordinarily such changes involve the entire distributed lag (lag length and lag coefficients) and the constant term. Easiest to identify is a structural shift wherein only the constant term undergoes significant change, with the distributed lag itself remaining statistically unchanged. Most difficult to identify is a change in lag length simply because the usual estimation procedures require that the correct lag length (usually unknown a priori) be specified in advance and also because the estimation procedures themselves are sensitive to lag length misspecification.

In the usual case, a complete sensitivity analysis is required to identify the correct prestructural change lag length specification. Since ordinarily several years or more will be required for a structural change to work its way through a distributed lag model (especially if the lag is several years long), a portion of the prechange sample period will not be available for the necessary sensitivity testing required to identify the correct prechange model. Where the available prechange period is short (mid-1950s to early 1960s) and the lag is fairly long (2½ years), the available sample will not be sufficiently long for sensitivity testing to identify the correct lag specification, let alone reliable estimation. It is not surprising, then, that the 1956-1962 Almon estimation of the 10-quarter-lag M_1 model is not significant (see Table 3A-2). Note that the 1956-1962 period leaves but 19 degrees of freedom after allowance for those lost in estimation, hardly adequate for a reliable estimation. Also, if the change took place over several years, the available sample period, say 1956-1960, would simply be too short to provide for any reliable model estimation whatsoever. To identify the structural change, the only alternative is to work backward into the 1956-1962 sample period with the known correct (for 1963-1971) 10-quarter-lag M_1 model and then test for changes in the distributed lag.

To identify the pre-1963 structural changes, our testing procedure makes use of a dummy variable on the constant and another different dummy variable on the individual lag coefficients of the 10-quarter-lag M_1 model. The dummies are formed in the usual fashion, taking values of 1 for the 1956/1-1963/1 sample period and 0 thereafter, implying that they do not apply for the latter period (1963/2-1971/2). The required estimations for our test, using the Almon method for convenience, are presented in Table 3-5. (For reference the 1956-1971 estimation without dummy variables is included at the bottom of the table.)

The interesting finding from adding a dummy constant is that the basic features of the 10-quarter uniform lag model remain statistically unchanged, and that the dummy itself is statistically identical in size, but opposite in sign, to the constant term. (This is the first estimation in Table 3-5.) Each distributed lag coefficient is significant; the sum of coefficients, 1.34, and constant, −2.3, are statistically identical to the previously obtained values of 1.42 and −2.6, respectively, for the 1963/2-1971/2 sample

Table 3-5
Structural Change Tests, 10-Quarter-Lag M_1 Model, 1956-1971

Lag Length	*R^2/SE*	*Durbin-Watson Statistic*	*Sum of Coefficients (t Value)*	*Periods with Significant Coefficients*	*Constant Term (t Value)*	*Dummy Sum of Coefficients (t Value)*	*Significant Dummy Coefficients*	*Dummy Constant (t Value)*
10	.62/1.05	1.85	1.34 (8.26)	0-10	−2.32 (−3.11)	–	–	2.19 (4.13)
11	.60/1.07	1.91	1.35 (8.03)	0-10	−2.25 (−3.08)	–	–	2.21 (4.06)
16	.64/1.02	2.06	1.34 (8.32)	All except 15, 16	−1.94 (−2.56)	–	–	1.72 (3.06)
30	.70/.93	2.49	1.48 (9.63)	All except 25-30	−2.00 (−3.19)	–	–	1.23 (2.46)
10	.61/1.05	1.99	1.36 (8.14)	0-10	−2.37 (−3.13)	−.34 (−.69)	None	2.80 (2.60)
10	.57/1.10	1.74	1.06 (8.28)	1-10	−.98 (−1.73)	.78 (3.14)	2-6	–
10	.51/1.19		0.82 (6.91)	1-10	−0.20 (−0.54)	–	–	–

period. When added, the dummy constant, 2.2 and the constant, −2.3, statistically cancel out, implying that the model shifted downward by about 2.5 percentage points in the early 1960s. For the 1956-1962 sample period, the constant is zero.

It is instructive to compare estimations with and without the dummy constant (last estimation in Table 3-5). Without the constant, the basic characteristics of the previously robust model have been completely submerged; for the 1956-1971 period the sum of coefficients is now 0.8, the constant is not significant, and R^2 has declined to 0.57. With a dummy constant, R^2 is 0.62 and the basic model is preserved. Note that this test assumes that an instantaneous shift occurred in 1963/1, when it is highly likely that the shift occurred over a period of time. Were we able to specify the shift dynamics, no doubt R^2 would improve. With additional resources, it would be useful to test a phasing-in process for the dummy constant.

The same results are obtained if the sample period is moved back one year to begin in 1955. The R^2/SE is 0.61/1.03, the sum of coefficients is 1.418(8.2), the constant is −2.67(−3.37), and the dummy constant is 3.22(3.11). Note that the sum of coefficients and the constant are *identical* with those obtained for the 1963/2-1971/2 sample period—an unusual result. Moving backward until 1954 finds an increase in the standard error to 1.21, but that reflects M_1 growth figures in mid-1951.

To test whether the lag is correctly specified at 10 quarters for the earlier period, the dummy constant is retained, but an eleventh lag is added (second estimation in Table 3-5). Statistically, the model is unchanged, except that the additional lag is nonsignificant. Even when the lag is extended to 16 or even 30 quarters (third and fourth estimations in Table 3-5), the basic features—the sum of coefficients and constant—remain unchanged. Some additional lag coefficients do become significant, but the redistribution of coefficients reflects the sensitivity of the Almon method to incorrect lag specification. This test confirms that 10 quarters is the correct lag length specification.

To test whether the distributed lag coefficients are identical between earlier and later sample periods, a dummy variable is added on each lag coefficient while the dummy constant (fifth estimation in Table 3-5) is retained. Again, the model is statistically unchanged; the individual dummy coefficients and their sum are not significant (the dummy sum is −0.34 with a *t* statistic value of only 0.7). When the dummy constant is excluded but the dummy on the coefficients is retained, the basic characteristics of the model are significantly changed. Statistically, the constant becomes zero and the sum of coefficients changes to 1; also R^2 declines to 0.57, and the current quarter's lag coefficient is no longer significant. These estimations imply that the lag coefficients appropriate for the 1963-1971 period apply to the earlier sample period as well, provided a dummy constant is specified.[7]

c. The Complete M_1 Model Estimations

Our estimation of the 10-quarter uniform lag M_1 model is now complete. For comparative purposes, the representative M_1 model estimations are presented in Table 3-6. Well almost! As a check on using the GNP implicit price deflator, the M_1 model was reestimated using the gross private domestic product (GPDP) deflator. Statistically the results were identical. In addition to the previously reported estimation through 1976, the estimations with the dummy constant for 1956-1971 and for the entire 20-year sample period (1956-1976) are included. Statistically, the sum of coefficients is identical for all four estimations. The principal difference lies in explanatory power. For the 1963-1971 period, R^2 is 0.78. When extended forward to 1976 or backward to 1956, R^2 drops to 0.65; the loss in explanatory power is apparently symmetrical on either side of 1963-1971.[8] For two decades then, the 10-quarter-lag M_1 monetarist inflation model (accounting for a structural shift) explains almost 70 percent of the variability in inflation—rather decent for a simple macroeconomic model that does not make visible the interactions of the monetary impulse upon real output.

d. Examining the Structural Shift of the Early 1960s

It is certainly not surprising that a structural change in the M_1 model does occur during our sample period of approximately two decades. We would not expect that accounting only for the direct effects of the monetary impulse upon prices would yield a stable relationship over long periods. What is surprising is that the M_1-price elasticity appears stable over two decades and that the shift comes about so abruptly. On casual inspection the shift

Table 3-6
Comparative 10-Quarter-Lag M_1 Model Estimations, 1956-1976

	1956-1971/2	*1963/2-1971/2*	*1956-1976/2*	*1963/2-1976/2*[a]
R^2/SE	0.62/1.05	0.78/0.81	0.65/1.55	0.63/1.63
Sum of Coefficients (*t* Value)	1.34 (8.3)	1.42 (10.4)	1.53 (8.9)	1.55 (8.4)
Periods with Significant Coefficients	All	All	1-10	2-10
Constant (*t* Value)	−2.3 (−3.1)	−2.7 (−4.3)	−2.8 (−3.2)	−2.9 (−2.9)
Dummy Constant (*t* Value)	2.2 (4.1)	–	2.4 (3.5)	–

[a]The Shiller estimation is essentially identical, except for the R^2 of 0.67.

does not seem associated with any corresponding change in the real economy. However, there was a change in the way reserve requirements were computed, and during this phasing-in process real cash balances declined for three quarters in succession. These changes are worth investigating to determine whether a more orderly shift adjustment can be identified.

Currency in bank vaults was allowed to count as legal reserves on a phased-in-basis, beginning December 1, 1959. Final phasing-in of the vault cash allotment was completed on November 23, 1960. During this phasing-in process, real balances declined as three quarters of negative M_1 growth rates were posted for the 1959/4-1960/2 period (−2.5, −1.8, and −0.7percent, respectively). Negative M_1 growth rates are clearly the exception in the postwar period; the last posted was −0.5 percent in 1966/3. Note that when the initial sample point was extended backward from 1963/2 by quarters, the shift is first noticeable beginning with a 1962/4 initial sample point. The elasticity becomes statistically proportional, and R^2 drops to 0.71.[9] With that initial sample point, the first quarter of M_1 growth that enters into the estimation is 1960/2 with its negative 0.7 percent figure.

To determine whether the three-quarter sequence of negative M_1 growth rates affects the shift adjustment, they were arbitrarily altered to a nominal positive value, 0.1, and the M_1 model was reestimated. (In effect, a dummy was introduced for three quarters.) Several changes are immediately apparent. The constant term, which previously became nonsignificant when the initial sample point was extended backward to 1961/2, now retains significance back to 1958. Also, the current period's lag coefficient, previously nonsignificant beginning with a 1962 initial sample point, also retains significance through 1958. And R^2 is several percentage points higher with the three-quarter M_1 growth data adjustment. These significant changes do suggest a more orderly shift adjustment of the 10-quarter uniformly weighted lag M_1 model during the early 1960s. To be sure, they do not explain the shift, but they do focus on an institutional change involving the computation of reserve balances that appears to be associated with an unusual three-quarter sequence of declining real balances.

3.7 Testing Causality Direction

Having completed estimating the M_1 model, we now inquire whether the causality direction was correctly specified. This is an especially important task for two reasons. First, a major claim of the monetarist inflation thesis is that causality runs predominantly from changes in money growth to changes in inflation. Second, our previous estimations of the 10-quarter-lag M_1 model or any other distributed lag are valid only if causality is unidirectional and correctly specified in the hypothesized direction. It is an advantage to make these causality tests after the M_1 model has been already examined.

The basic idea in a Sims test of Granger causality, as applied to our study, is that to support the null hypothesis of unidirectional causality running from changes in money growth to changes in inflation, then in a statistically significant regression of past and future lags of money growth on, i.e. explaining, inflation, the future lag coefficients should not be significant.[10] The major concerns are first ensuring the significance of the regression and second correctly assessing the *real* significance of the future lag coefficients. Typically four regressions are made for a homogeneous sample period. In addition to the regression discussed above, the reverse is run (past and future lags of inflation on money growth), together with future lags of money growth on inflation and its reverse regression, future lags of inflation on money growth. Sims suggested that four future and eight past lags would be suitable.

Functionally, the regressions are written as follows:

$$p_t = f(m_{t+4}, \ldots, m_{t+1}, m_t, m_{t-1}, \ldots, m_{t-8}) \tag{3.2}$$

$$p_t = g(m_{t+4}, \ldots, m_{t+1}, m_t) \tag{3.3}$$

$$m_t = h(p_{t+4}, \ldots, p_{t+1}, p_t, p_{t-1}, \ldots, p_{t-8}) \tag{3.4}$$

$$m_t = j(p_{t+4}, \ldots, p_{t+1}, p_t) \tag{3.5}$$

It is readily seen that functionally equations (3.2) and (3.3) are symmetric mirror images of Equations (3.4) and (3.5). In (3.2) and (3.4) the roles of m and p are reversed, and also in (3.3) and (3.5).

The first prerequisite is determining whether the regressions involving past and future lags are statistically significant; otherwise, the Sims test cannot be made. Ordinarily there will not be a strong underlying distributed lag model involving just past lags; the addition of future lags, or future lags only, almost inevitably means that the lag is *misspecified.* This is not a trifling matter, since the conventional distributed lag estimation techniques are reliable *only* if the correct lag length is specified in advance, and they are subject to lag misspecifiation error. The usual prescription is to not rely on only one estimation method, lest the test results be estimation-dependent.

A Sims/Granger test, then, involves correctly interpreting coefficients from misspecified distributed lag time-series regressions. Careful use of the F statistic is required before assigning significance to a regression. Since the expected F test values will often be fairly low and the test is dependent on serially uncorrelated estimation residuals, the data are often prefiltered to yield only white noise; spectral density tests are then typically employed to examine the residuals. (The Durbin-Watson statistic is not completely suitable.) Since our data are expressed as growth rates (Δ log p and Δ log m), the prefiltering was omitted. Resource limitations precluded assessing the significance of this omission, but partial amends, if any are required, are made by choosing small F test critical regions (less than 1 percent).

In specifying the number of past and future lags, Sims suggested that four future and eight past lags would ordinarily be sufficiently generous. However, if the "true" past lag exceeds eight periods, then a constraint is in effect imposed and may "push" significance upon one or more future lag coefficients. Since it has already been determined that the M_1 model is correctly specified with a 10-quarter lag, we have the opportunity to observe the effects of a past lag constraint by specifying eight past lags and then relaxing the constraint. The M_1 model is a good test model of the sensitivity of the Sims procedure to lag constraints. Its weights are uniform, it is not estimation-dependent, and it is powerful.

Another considertion is ensuring sample homogeneity. Ordinarily, the usual practice is to apply a Chou test on the lag coefficients. However, the confidence intervals on distributed lag coefficients are apt to be fairly wide, and there will be typically a good deal of uncertainty about the population distributed lag. Since we already have completely determined the characteristics of the M_1 model for the 1956-1976 sample period, it is sensible to use that detailed information and make Sims tests for each of four sample periods: 1963-1971 (known stability), 1956-1971 (stable except for a structural shift), 1963-1976 (stable but unusual nonmonetary price effects), and the entire sample period. In all, some 16 regressions are initially used to test the null hypothesis of unidirectional causality running from changes in M_1 growth to changes in inflation.

To assess the significance of future lag coefficients, we depend on the t statistic ratios, size relative to significant past lag coefficients, and placement. Relatively large but nonsignificant future lag coefficients (compared to past lag ones) merit careful attention. Also, significant but relatively small-sized future lag coefficients need not necessarily be meaningful. Placement matters, too; more attention is given to the size of the third and fourth future lag coefficients than to the first or second.

The summary results of the Sims/Granger tests are presented in Table 3-7. In this table are presented the F test values of the 16 regressions (four each for four periods) together with adjoining parentheses denoting significant future lag coefficients by their position, if any, and a letter (S or L) designating whether the significant future lag coefficients are large or small in size relative to the significant past lag coefficients. A single asterisk adjoining the bracket denotes that the F test value is significant at a 1 percent level; two asterisks denote significance at a 5 percent level. The complete 16 estimations with individual coefficient values appear in Tables 3A-8 through 3A-10.

Table 3-7
Sims Causality Test Summary Results for M_1

		F Statistics			
		$\dot{M}_1$ *on* $\dot{P}$		$\dot{P}$ *on* $\dot{M}_1$	
Degrees of Freedom	*Sample Period*	*Past and Future Lags*	*Future Lags*	*Past and Future Lags*	*Future Lags*
F(4/53)	1956-1971	12.9*(3, 4, S)	2.2	14.1* (1-4, L)	8.7* (3, 4, L)
F(4/24)	1963-1971	14.4*(1, 2, S)	1.1	3.1** (1-3)	3.5** (2, 3, L)
F(4/46)	1963-1976	14.2*	0.2	2.2 (1)	2.0
F(4/73)	1956-1976	26.1*(3, 4, S)	2.4	12.3* (2-4, L)	8.9* (3, L)

Significance Levels	*1 Percent*	*5 Percent*
F(4/53)	3.70	2.57
F(4/24)	4.22	2.78
F(4/46)	3.78	2.60
F(4/73)	3.61	2.52

Estimations made with Almon method, third-degree polynomial. For future lag regressions, four future lags and current lag are used. For future and past lag regressions, four future, current, and eight past lags are used. M_1 and P measured in annualized quarterly growth rates. Complete test results in Tables 3A-8 to 3A-10.

*denotes significance at 1 percent test value

**denotes significance at 5 percent test value

( ) denotes significant future lag coefficients. Letter S or L denotes relatively small or large coefficients compared to significant past lag coefficients.

The first requirement calls for significant regressions involving past and future lags. Of the 16 estimations, eight are significant at 1 percent and 2 others at 5 percent test levels. Each of the four regressions of past and future M_1 growth on (explaining) inflation are highly significant, with *F* values greatly surpassing the 1 percent test levels. However, none of the four regressions of future M_1 growth on (explaining) inflation are significant; this result indirectly supports the null hypothesis.

Turning to the future lag coefficients, when future and past lags of M_1 growth are regressed on inflation, two relatively small future lag coefficients are significant in three of the four regressions. To test the impact of the eight-period lag constraint, an additional lag was allowed for the 1963-1971 period. Not unexpectedly, only the small-sized first future lag coefficient remained significant, implying that the 8 past lag constraint was "pushing" future lags into significance. This is a nice illustration that a knowledge of the "true" lag may be helpful in correctly conducting Sims/Granger tests.

When the past lag was extended to 10 periods, the first future lag coefficient still remained significant but not the tenth past lag coefficient. If a uniform lag model estimation can easily "slide" between a past lag and one or two future lag coefficients, this suggests that more than the usual caution is needed before giving significance to future lag coefficients. And, as noted before, none of the four regressions of future lags of M_1 growth on inflation were significant. Together, these regressions of M_1 growth on inflation support the null hypothesis.

Looking at the reverse regressions of past and future inflation on (explaining) M_1 growth, we find that highly significant *F* values are obtained for periods 1956-1971 and 1956-1976. In the first period, all four future lag coefficients are large and significant; for the entire sample period, three future lag coefficients are large and significant. When future inflation alone is regressed on M_1 growth, highly significant *F* values are again obtained for these periods. For 1956-1971, two future lag coefficients (3 and 4) are large and significant; for the entire period, the third future lag coefficient is large and significant. Also, the two regressions for the 1963-1971 period that are significant at the 5 percent test level each have at least two significant future lag coefficients. Taken together, the results of these reverse regressions strongly reject unidirectional causality running from changes in inflation to changes in the M_1 growth and by inference support the null hypothesis.

The Sims/Granger test results strongly support the null hypothesis of unidirectional causality running from changes in M_1 growth to changes in inflation. The estimations previously made in this chapter are valid insofar as the causality direction was correctly specified. There is at least one specification of money, then, that strongly supports the bold monetarist claim that changes in money growth causes changes in inflation. The test results do not "prove" one-way causality; rather, they show that it is *possible* and reject the possibility that it goes in the opposite direction.

Notes

1. See Andersen and Karnosky (1972) and Karnosky (1976). Other lag specifications have been suggested: Gordon (1975) suggests 28, Levy (1975) suggests 15, Selden (1977) suggests 13, Keran (1975) suggests 12. Since none of these studies reported the results of any sensitivity or causality direction analyses (both standard econometric procedures), the diversity of lag length specifications is not surprising.

L. Andersen and D. Karnosky, "The Appropriate Time Frames for Controlling Monetary Aggregates: The St. Louis Evidence," in *Controlling Monetary Aggregates II: The Implementation,* Conference Series No. 9, (Federal Reserve Bank of Boston, September 1972), pp. 147-177; D. Karnosky, "The Link between Money and Prices, 1971-1976," *Review* of the Federal Reserve Bank of St. Louis, June 1976, pp. 17-23; M. Levy, "Constraining Inflation: Causes, Complacencies and Evidence," *The Con-*

ference Board Record 12, no. 10, pp. 8-14; R. Selden, "Inflation: Are We Winning the Fight?" *The Morgan Guaranty Survey*, October 1977, pp. 7-13; M. Keran, "Toward an Explanation of Simultaneous Inflation-Recession," *Business Review* of the Federal Reserve Bank of San Francisco, Spring 1975, pp. 18-30.

2. These and subsequent estimations in this chapter, unless otherwise specified, are made with a third-degree Almon procedure without any other constraints. Most Almon estimations are made with a third- or fourth-degree polynomial. Some experimentation showed a third-degree polynomial was not inferior to a fourth-degree one.

3. A priori, we do not have any information about the values of the initial lag coefficients, i.e. whether they should be included. The appropriate test is whether they should be constrained to zero. However, the Cargill-Meyer Monte Carlo simulation study finds that the Almon procedure is sensitive to initial lag constraint misspecification error, stating that "Unless specific a priori information is available, the Almon procedure should not be constrained." See T. Cargill and R. Meyer, "Some Time and Frequency Domain Distributed Lag Estimators: A Comparative Monte Carlo Study," *Econometrica* 42, no. 6 (November 1974): 1031-44.

4. Disaggregating the major explanatory variables and retesting the model is a standard sensitivity analysis technique. For example, see S. Goldfeld, "The Demand for Money Revisited," *BPEA* 3 (1973): 612-63. Note that we do not a priori require that both demand-deposit and currency monetarist inflation models have identical lag specifications and elasticities, but we do require that they can be correctly specified in a not too dissimilar fashion from the M_1 model.

5. Interestingly, the OLS R^2 estimate is 0.85 compared with the Almon/Shiller estimates of 0.78, confirming the conventional wisdom that OLS-distributed lag estimations give biased standard errors. The usual reference on the bias of OLS estimators for distributed lag model estimations with small samples is J. Johnson, *Econometric Methods* (New York: McGraw-Hill, 1963), pp. 211-21. Whether the Cargill and Meyer findings would hold for a uniform distribution is unknown.

6. Goldfeld (1976) adopts this view by inference, whereas Hamburgher (1977) claims that the demand for money has simply been incorrectly specified and, by implication, that the recent changes are not quantitatively important as regards the money demand equation. S. Goldfeld, "The Case of the Missing Money," *BPEA* 3 (1976): 638-730; M. Hamburgher, "Behavior of the Money Stock: Is There a Puzzle?" *Journal of Monetary Economics* (July 1977): 265 *ff.* Also, Jessup and Bochnak note that between 1971 and 1975 more than 30 money-market mutual funds had been established with aggregate assets exceeding $7 billion and over 150,000 participants. See P. Jessup and M. Bocknak, "Money Market Mutual Funds:

Their Impact on Banks," *Bank Administration* (September 1977): 28-32.

7. We can now explain why Selden ("Inflation: Are We Winning the Fight?"), Karnosky ("The Link between Money and Prices"), and Andersen and Karnosky ("Appropriate Time Frames for Controlling Monetry Aggregates") found a unit M_1-price elasticity. They ignored the shift in the early 1960s.

8. The Shiller estimate for the 1963/2-1976/2 sample period has a 1.54 sum of coefficients, a constant of −2.9, and an R^2 of 0.67. All coefficients are significant save those for periods 0 and 1.

9. The estimates are as follows:

Initial Sample Point	R^2/SE	*Elasticity*	*Constant*
1963/2	.78/.81	1.4	−2.7
1963/1	.77/.80	1.3	−2.4
1962/4	.71/.90	1.2	−1.7
1962/3	.72/.92	1.2	−1.4
1962/2	.71/.93	1.1	−1.1

10. C. Sims, "Money, Income and Causality," *American Economic Review* 62, no. 4 (September 1972): 540-52; C.W.J. Granger, "Investigating Causal Relations by Econometric Models and Cross Spectral Models," *Econometrica* 37 (July 1969): 424-38.

Appendix 3A Complete Sensitivity Analyses and Causality Test Results for the M_1 Monetarist Inflation Model

Table 3A-1
Overlapping Sample Sensitivity Tests, 20-Quarter-Lag M_1 Model, 1956-1971

Sample Period	*Sum of Coefficients (t-Value)*	R^2/SE	*Durbin-Watson Statistic*	*Periods with Significant Coefficients*
1956/2-1962/2	1.984 (2.10)	.37/1.05	3.05[a]	15-19
1957/2-1963/2[b]	.658 (.46)	−.08/1.08	2.46	–
1958/2-1964/2[b]	−.855 (−.66)	.01/.96	2.46	–
1959/2-1965/2[b]	.470 (.58)	−.08/.97	2.52	–
1960/2-1966/2[b]	1.309 (2.79)	.36/.96	2.49	–
1961/2-1967/2	.685 (1.67)	.14/1.01	2.32	–
1962/2-1968/2	1.219 (5.57)	.57/.90	2.34	0-3, 10-17
1963/2-1969/2	1.248 (6.43)	.66/.89	2.42	0-10
1964/2-1970/2	1.149 (4.42)	.69/.86	2.51	–
1965/2-1971/2	1.367 (4.97)	.59/.89	2.16	13, 14

[a]Denotes positive serial correlation.

[b]Denotes F test is not significant.

Table 3A-2
Overlapping Sample Sensitivity Tests, 10-Quarter-Lag M_1 Model, 1956-1971

Sample Period	*Sum of Coefficients (t-Value)*	*R^2/SE*	*Durbin-Watson Statistic*	*Periods with Significant Coefficients*
[a]1956/2-1962/2	.926 (1.54)	–.05/1.35	1.75	–
[a]1957/2-1963/2	–.015 (–.03)	–.02/1.04	2.60	–
[a]1958/2-1964/2	–.005 (–.01)	.06/.92	2.74[b]	–
[a]1959/2-1965/2	.203 (.70)	.03/.92	2.84[b]	–
1960/2-1966/2	.616 (2.84)	.28/1.01	2.22	2, 3
[a]1961/2-1967/2	.579 (2.85)	.18/.98	2.38	3, 4, 5
1962/2-1968/2	.949 (4.09)	.48/.98	1.95	1, 2, 3
1963/2-1969/2	1.329 (6.68)	.68/.85	2.63	All
1964/2-1970/2	1.473 (7.59)	.70/.84	2.74[b]	All
1965/2-1971/2	1.634 (7.20)	.68/.79	2.43	All

[a]Denotes F test is not significant.
[b]Denotes positive serial correlation.

Table 3A-3
Sideways Straddle Sensitivity Tests, 10-Quarter-Lag M_1 Model, 1963-1971

Lag Specification	*Sum of Coefficients (t Value)*	*R^2/SE*	*Durbin-Watson Statistic*	*Periods with Significant Coefficients*	*Constant Term (t Value)*
0-10	1.42 (10.46)	.78/.81	2.58	0-10	–2.67 (–4.29)
1-11	1.39 (10.12)	.76/.84	2.82	1-11	–2.45 (–4.00)
2-12	1.28 (10.23)	.77/.82	2.42	2-4, 6-11	–1.89 (–3.43)
3-13	1.11 (7.54)	.63/1.04	1.79	3-5, 7-12	–0.92 (–1.45)

Table 3A-4
Straddle Sensitivity Tests, 5 Semiannual Lag M_1 Model, 1963-1971

	Lags		
	2 Years	*2.5 Years*	*3 Years*
Sum of Coefficients (*t* value)	1.238 (9.24)	1.269 (10.87)	1.305 (10.61)
R^2/SE	0.848/0.60	0.884/0.52	0.882/0.53
Constant (*t* value)	−1.929 (−3.15)	−1.949 (−3.65)	−2.22 (−3.74)
Lag Coefficients			
0	0.267 (3.43)	0.203 (2.82)	0.283 (3.30)
1	0.242 (3.93)	0.207 (4.30)	0.187 (4.61)
2	0.171 (3.60)	0.205 (5.26)	0.199 (5.18)
3	0.177 (2.92)	0.204 (4.80)	0.250 (7.28)
4	0.383 (5.34)	0.212 (4.38)	0.269 (5.95)
5		0.238 (3.43)	0.186 (5.23)
6			0.069 (0.80)

Table 3A-5
Complete Shiller and Almon Estimations, 10-Quarter-Lag M_1 Model, 1963-1971

Regression Statistics	*Almon*	*Shiller*
Constant (t value)	−2.67 (−4.29)	−2.71 (−4.43)
Lag Period Coefficients (t value)		
0	0.16 (3.31)	0.16 (4.19)
1	0.15 (5.92)	0.15 (5.75)
2	0.14 (5.45)	0.13 (6.30)
3	0.12 (4.80)	0.12 (6.23)
4	0.11 (4.94)	0.11 (6.05)
5	0.10 (5.01)	0.10 (6.08)
6	0.09 (4.21)	0.11 (6.30)
7	0.10 (3.88)	0.12 (6.74)
8	0.12 (4.86)	0.13 (7.22)
9	0.15 (6.61)	0.15 (6.67)
10	0.20 (4.31)	0.16 (4.59)
$\sum_{i=0}^{10} w_i$	1.42 (10.43)	1.43
SE/R^2	0.81/0.78	0.80/0.79
Durbin-Watson Statistic	2.58	2.57
Simulation Statistics (1971/3-1976/2)		
RMSE	2.72	2.70
MAE	2.19	2.18

Table 3A-6
Almon Estimation Residuals, 10-Quarter-Lag M_1 Model, 1963-1971

Quarter	*(1)* *Actual Inflation*	*(2)* *Predicted Inflation*	*(1) – (2)* *Residual*
1963/2	0.3	0.5	–0.3
3	1.2	1.1	0.1
4	2.7	1.5	1.2
1964/1	1.2	1.3	–0.2
2	1.4	1.5	–0.2
3	2.2	1.7	0.5
4	0.8	1.9	–1.1
1965/1	3.3	1.8	1.4
2	2.1	2.5	–0.5
3	2.7	2.9	–0.2
4	1.9	3.3	–1.4
1966/1	4.0	3.7	0.3
2	4.7	3.8	0.9
3	2.3	3.0	–0.6
4	3.7	2.8	0.9
1967/1	2.4	2.9	–0.6
2	1.5	2.7	–1.3
3	3.9	3.4	0.5
4	4.6	4.0	0.5
1968/1	5.1	4.5	0.6
2	4.6	5.1	–0.5
3	3.7	5.1	–1.4
4	5.6	4.9	0.7
1969/1	4.3	4.6	–0.3
2	5.1	5.1	0
3	6.2	5.5	0.7
4	4.9	5.4	–0.5
1970/1	6.0	5.3	0.7
2	4.9	4.7	0.2
3	3.6	4.8	–1.2
4	5.4	5.2	0.2
1971/1	6.0	5.3	0.8
2	5.6	5.6	0

The figures have been rounded off; hence the residual figures may not always agree with the difference between the middle two columns.

Table 3A-7
Backward Lengthening Sample Sensitivity Tests, 10-Quarter-Lag M_1 Model, 1956-1971

Initial Sample Point	R^2/SE	*Sum of Coefficients (t Value)*	*Periods with Significant Coefficients*	*Constant (t Value)*
1963/2	0.78/.81	1.42 (10.43)	0-10	−2.67 (−4.29)
1962/2	0.71/.93	1.10 (9.02)	1-10	−1.13 (−2.12)
1961/2	0.68/.99	0.99 (8.98)	1-10	−0.60 (−1.29)
1960/2	0.70/.99	1.01 (10.17)	1-10	−0.70 (−1.76)
1959/2	0.65/1.03	0.93 (9.21)	1-10	−0.35 (−0.94)
1958/2	0.64/1.04	0.86 (9.18)	1-10	−0.03 (−0.08)
1957/2	0.58/1.12	0.81 (8.67)	1-10	0.23 (0.71)
1956/2	0.51/1.19	0.82 (7.27)	1-10	0.20 (0.54)

1971/2 is the sample endpoint.

Table 3A-8
Sims Tests, 1963-1971

Coefficient on Lag	$\dot{M}_1$ *on* $\dot{P}$		$\dot{P}$ *on* $\dot{M}_1$		$\dot{M}_2$ *on* $\dot{P}$		$\dot{P}$ *on* $\dot{M}_2$		*Time Deposits on* $\dot{P}$		$\dot{P}$ *on Time Deposits*		*Total Reserves on* $\dot{P}$		$\dot{P}$ *on Total Reserves*	
+4	.02	–	.37	–.57	.12	–	.79	–.47	–.02	–.02	1.25*	–.40	.21	.33	.40*	.03
+3	.05	.24	.51*	.66*	.03	.05	.67*	.82*	–.05*	–.02	.82*	.93	.15	–.04	.35*	.20
+2	.07*	–.03	.53*	.79*	–.01	–.06	.51*	.76*	–.06*	–.03	.45	.66	.13*	–.08	.27*	.25
+1	.09*	–.20	.43*	.25	–.02	–.15	.31	–.08	–.07*	–.06	.14	–.50	.13*	–	.15	.06
0	.10*	.31	.26	.53	–	–.03	.11	–1.12*	–.07*	–.15	–.11	–1.87*	.16*	.01	.03	–.46
–1	.11*		.05		.04		–.10*		–.06*		–.31		.20*		–.10	
–2	.11*		–.16		.09*		.29*		–.05*		–.46*		.25*		–.21*	
–3	.12*		–.35*		.14*		–.45*		–.05		–.58*		.29*		–.29*	
–4	.12*		–.48*		.19*		–.56*		–.05		–.66*		.32*		–.33*	
–5	.13*		–.52*		.21*		–.61*		–.05		–.72*		.33*		–.31*	
–6	.14*		–.44*		.22*		–.58*		–.06		–.74*		.32*		–.23*	
–7	.15*		–.21		.18*		–.46*		–.08		–.76*		.27*		–.06	
–8	.17*		–.22		.11*		–.22		–.11		–.76*		.18		.20	
SE/R^2	.98/.66	1.67/–	1.92/.28	1.93/.27	1.31/0.38	1.68/–	2.20/0.38	2.54/0.17	1.32/0.38	1.47/0.22	3.18/0.51	3.94/.25	1.08/.58	1.71/–	1.29/.24	1.48/–
Σw_i	1.37(.21)	–	.18(.34)	.60(.28)	1.32(.45)	–	–0.90(.39)	–0.09(.37)	–.77(.24)	–.28(.10)	–2.44(.57)	–1.18(.55)	2.95(.63)	–	–.12(.23)	–
F(4/24)	14.40**	1.10	3.7	3.5	5.33**	0.89	5.34**	2.47	5.24**	3.03	8.18**	3.29	10.76**	0.71	3.19	.96

Sample period is 1963/2-1970/2 (allows 1971/2 endpoint); parentheses denote standard errors; variables are expressed in quarterly rates of growth at annual rates.

*denotes significant coefficient; t value $\geqslant 2$.

**denotes significant F. F(4/24) = 4.2 at 1 percent.

Table 3A-9
Sims Tests, 1963-1976

Coefficient on Lag	$\dot{M}_1$ on $\dot{P}$		$\dot{P}$ on $\dot{M}_1$		$\dot{M}_2$ on $\dot{P}$		$\dot{P}$ on $\dot{M}_2$		Time Deposits on $\dot{P}$		$\dot{P}$ on Time Deposits		Total Member Bank Reserves on $\dot{P}$		$\dot{P}$ on Total Member Bank Reserves	
+4	–.14	–.12	.10	.01	.05	.12	.16	–.03	–		.20	–.11	–.05	.37	.01	.09
+3	–.07	.07	.10*	.24	.05	.03	.08	.27	–.01	.08	.03	.26	.01	.11	.07*	.03
+2	–.01	–.03	.07	.25	.04	–.05	.01	.20	–.02	–.03	–.07	.16	.05	–.01	.09*	.15
+1	.02	–.12	.03	.05	.04	.06	–.03	–.04	–.03	–.05	–.12	–.13	.08	.08	.08	.19
0	.04	–.08	–.01	–.34	.04	.06	–.06	–.26	–.04	–.03	–.13	–.32	.10	.44	.05	–.07
–1	.05		–.06		.04		–.08		–.04	–.04	–.11		.11*		–	
–2	.06*		–.10*		.04		–.08		–.04		–.06		.12*		–.04	
–3	.08*		–.11		.05		–.06		–.03		–.01		.13*		–.07	
–4	.10*		–.11		.07		–.03		–.03		.04		.14*		–.07	
–5	.13*		–.06		.09*		.01		–.02		.08		.16*		–.04	
–6	.19*		.02		.13*		.07		–.02		.09		.19*		.03	
–7	.27*		.16		.17*		.14		–.01		.07		.24*		.16*	
–8	.38*		.36		.22*		.22		–		–.01		.31*		.36*	
SE/R^2	1.89/0.51	2.80/–	2.19/.09	2.21/.08	2.43/.20	2.8/–	2.8/–	2.8/–	2.77/–	2.78/–	4.33/–	4.32/–	1.92/.51	2.50/.16	1.58/.27	1.67/.19
Σw_i	1.11(.27)	–	.40(.19)	.20(.14)	1.04(.32)	–	.37(.24)	.14(.18)	–	–	–	–	1.59(.24)	.98(.27)	.64(.15)	.39(.10)
F(4/46)	14.2**	.21	2.23	2.0	4.20**	.26	1.1	.83	.51	.44	.39	.40	13.32**	3.37	5.51**	3.90**

Sample period is 1963/2-1975/4 (allows 1976/4 endpoint); parentheses denote standard errors; variables are expressed in quarterly rates of growth at annual rates.

*denotes significant coefficient; t value ⩾ 2.

**denotes significant F. F(4/46) = 3.8 at 1 percent.

Table 3A-10
Sims Tests, 1956-1971 and 1956-1976

Coefficient on Lag	$\dot{M}_1$ *on* $\dot{P}$ *1956-1971*		$\dot{P}$ *on* $\dot{M}_1$ *1956-1971*		$\dot{M}_1$ *on* $\dot{P}$ *1956-1976*		$\dot{P}$ *on* $\dot{M}_1$ *1956-1976*	
+4	–.10*	.02	.63*	.12	–.16*	.03	.27*	.23
+3	–.05*	.12	.50*	.73*	–.09*	.10	.20*	.38*
+2	–.01	–.05	.35*	.52*	–.03	.01	.12*	.24
+1	–.02	–.12	.19*	–	.01	–.01	.04	–.03
0	.04*	.27*	.03	–.36	.04	.26	–.03	–.25
–1	.06*		–.11		.06*		–.08*	
–2	.07*		–.23*		.07*		–.12*	
–3	.08*		–.31*		.09*		–.13*	
–4	.08*		–.33*		.10*		–.10	
–5	.09*		–.29*		.13*		–.04	
–6	.10*		–.18*		.16*		.07	
–7	.11*		.03		.20*		.24*	
–8	.12*		.34*		.26*		.47*	
SE/R^2	1.19/.46	1.55/.08	1.92/.48	2.14/35	1.72/.57	2.53/.07	2.24/.37	2.38/.29
Σw_i	.60(6.09)	–	.62(2.38)	1.00(4.84)	.84(7.99)	.39(2.91)	.90(5.49)	.57(5.04)
F(4/53)	12.91**	2.21	14.11**	8.66**				
F(4/73)					26.12**	2.42	12.26**	8.88**

Sample period 1956-1970/2 allows 1971/2 endpoint; sample period 1956-1975/2 allows 1976/2 endpoint; parentheses denote standard errors; variables are expressed in quarterly rates of growth, annualized.

*denotes significant coefficient; t value $\geqslant 2$.

**denotes significant F. F(4/53) = 3.7 at 1 percent; F(4/73) = 3.61 at 1 percent.

4 Specification Analysis of Money Aggregates Other than M_1

4.1 Introduction and Summary

In Chapter 3, attention was focused on the most common definition of money, M_1, which in a properly specified model did support the monetarist inflation thesis. Since the thesis does not specify how money should be defined, a careful study should cast a broad net over a variety of definitions. After all, it is the totality of the evidence that deserves attention. If the thesis is valid, it is not unreasonable to expect at least some support from other money specifications in addition to M_1, especially from the high-powered reserve aggregates. And if the broader M_2 aggregate gives poor results because of different inflation responses to the monetary impulse, as between interest- and non-interest-bearing deposits, we would also expect that M_3 will be found unacceptable for similar reasons.

The specifications examined in this chapter include the broader M_2 and M_3 aggregates (and by inference the M_4 and M_5 aggregates, respectively), three reserve aggregates—reserve base, total reserves, and nonborrowed reserves—and Niehans's recent suggestion of using changes in the Federal Reserve's government securities portfolio as a monetary measure. M_2 is defined as M_1 plus the time/savings deposits excluding negotiable CDs over \$100,000 at commercial banks. M_3 adds to M_2 the time/savings deposits at thrift institutions (mutual savings banks, savings and loan associations, and credit unions) and also excludes negotiable CDs over \$100,000. Total reserves include member bank vault cash holdings and deposits at Federal Reserve banks (held for purposes of fulfilling legal reserve requirements on time/savings and demand deposit liabilities). Nonborrowed reserves excludes from total reserves borrowings obtained from the Federal Reserve's short-term lending facility—the discount window. The reserve base adds public currency holdings outside banks to total reserves.

Our findings are as follows. Econometrically, M_2 and M_3 cannot be correctly specified in monetarist inflation models; their estimated lag distributions are unstable, and forward-simulation forecasts are poor. The origin for their unsatisfactory performance unambiguously lies with their major components; time/savings deposits at commercial banks and at thrifts (M_2-M_1 and M_3-M_2, respectively) cannot be correctly specified in a monetarist inflation model. Tests with M_2-M_1 find that causality runs in both directions. Interestingly, there is some causality support for M_2 in the hypothesized direction, but this is a spurious result, reflecting the combined influence of unidirectional causality for M_1 and the absence of supporting unidirectional causality for the much larger time/savings deposit component, M_2-M_1. Although not econometrically reliable, the estimated money-price elasticities (sum of distributed lag coefficients) for time/savings deposits are the same for both commercial banks and thrifts (M_2-M_1 and M_3-M_2), -0.7. They are one half the size of, but opposite in sign to, that for M_1. It is clear that the relationship between the growth of time/savings deposits and inflation requires a more complex modeling than can be provided by the single-equation monetarist inflation model requiring unidirectional causality.

On the basis of an incomplete sensitivity analysis and limited causality testing, nonborrowed reserves appear to be a suitable specification for a monetarist inflation model. A complete sensitivity analysis replicating that made for M_1 was far beyond the resources available to this study. However, our limited sensitivity analysis was encouraging and suggests that the strength of a reserve monetarist inflation model could be documented with further analysis. Sims/Granger tests for total reserves provide some support for the hypothesized unidirectional causality. Similar findings would be expected for nonborrowed reserves. A total reserves model is approximately correctly specified at 15 quarters with uniform weights. This model explains about 60 percent of the variance in inflation and has a unit elasticity for 1963-1971. The post-1971/2 out-of-sample forward-simulation forecasts are quite similar to, but less accurate than, those obtained with the 10-quarter-lag uniformly weighted M_1 model. The reserve base model was unsatisfactory because of aggregation problems; the currency-price elasticity is twice that of reserves. Also, Niehans's suggested specification was unsatisfactory.

In summary, specification analysis finds that M_1 is not a lone wolf. A reserve aggregate monetarist model with total or nonborrowed reserves gives promising results with inflation forecasts similar to those with M_1. Also, there is some support for unidirectional causality in the hypothesized direction for total reserves and, by inference, nonborrowed reserves. The popular broader M_2 and M_3 aggregates give poor results for readily identifiable reasons—changes in interest-bearing deposits (M_2-M_1 and M_3-M_2) do not have a unidirectional causal or econometrically reliable relationship with inflation. It is perhaps ironic, but not unexpected, that among the conventional monetary aggregates, the monetarist inflation thesis should hold strictly for M_1, considering that the broader aggregates, M_2 and M_3, have received increasing public attention in recent years.[1]

The order of presentation is as follows. In Section 4.2, a sensitivity and causality analysis of M_2 and its major component, M_2-M_1, is presented. An abbreviated sensitivity analysis of M_3 and its major component, M_3-M_2, is discussed in Section 4.3. The three reserve aggregates are examined in Section 4.4, and a causality analysis of total reserves is reported. Finally, Niehans's suggestion of using the Federal Reserve's government securities portfolio as a monetary measure is examined briefly in Section 4.5.

4.2 The M_2 Specification

a. Sensitivity Analysis

Replicating the procedure used with M_1, preliminary sensitivity analysis begins by arbitrarily specifying a 20-quarter lag and estimating that model for both the 1956-1971 sample period and the two previously selected subperiods, 1956-1965 and 1966-1971. For the entire sample period, the 20-quarter-lag M_2 model explains about one-half the variability in inflation; the M_2-price elasticity (sum of distributed lag coefficients) is about 0.7, and lag periods 9 through 20 have statistically significant coefficients. Since the first half of the distributed lag is not statistically significant, the M_2 model was reestimated with those lag periods constrained to zero. Statistically, the estimation is unchanged except that now only lag periods 13 through 19 have statistically significant coefficients. The implication that inflation is "explained" by changes in M_2 growth lagged three and four years is implausible.

Looking at the subperiods, we find that estimation for the first subperiod, ending in 1965, is not statistically significant. However, that for the second subperiod is significant but differs markedly with the estimation obtained for the entire sample period. The M_2-price elasticity is now twice as large, 1.7, and only lag periods 0, 1, and 16 to 20 have statistically significant coefficients. Once again, preliminary sensitivity analysis of a monetarist inflation model suggests that a 20-quarter lag is misspecified.

Since M_1 comprises about one-third of all M_2 deposits and the M_1 model had previously been found rigorously stable for the 1963-1971 sample period, it is a useful economy in which to temporarily restrict further sensitivity analysis with M_2 to that period.[2] An M_2 model that is stable for a much shorter sample period will not be interesting;promising results would obviously warrant extending the sample period.

An "economizing" lag sensitivity analysis of the M_2 model was made with lag specifications 9 through 15 quarters in length, and also for 20 quarters. The estimations and forward-simulation statistics are presented in Table 4-1. They unambiguously imply that M_2 cannot be correctly specified in a monetarist inflation model, although if the lag is made long enough, R^2 becomes respectable. The most noticeable feature of the estimations is that as the lag is lengthened, R^2 increases, but earlier statistically significant coefficients are lost as new ones are gained; the total number re-

Table 4-1
M_2 Monetarist Inflation Model Estimations, Variable Lags, 1963-1971

	Number of Lags								
	0-9	*0-10*	*0-11*	*0-12*	*0-13*	*0-14*	*0-15*	*0-20*	*10 to 20*
Regression Statistics									
R^2/SE	0.27/1.46	0.45/1.27	0.40/1.32	0.46/1.25	0.53/1.17	0.53/1.18	0.56/1.13	0.63/1.04	0.65/1.02
Sum of Coefficients	1.10	1.47	1.51	1.42	1.28	1.26	1.11	0.95	0.88
(*t* value)	(3.17)	(4.53)	(4.43)	(4.37)	(4.07)	(3.95)	(3.59)	(8.02)	(7.12)
Periods with Significant Coefficients	1, 7-9	1-2, 5-10	1, 4-11	4-12	5-13	6-13	7-14	9-20	11-19
Forward-Simulation Statistics									
(1971/3-1976/2)									
MAE	2.59	2.43	1.93	1.58	1.60	1.52	1.79	2.67	4.9
RMSE	3.09	2.78	2.41	2.17	2.11	2.03	2.19	3.22	6.00

Durbin-Watson statistics range from 1.07 for 9 lags to 1.82 for 20 lags.

mains fixed at about eight or nine. With a 20-quarter lag, R^2 is 0.63, but only the last half of the lag distribution is statistically significant. However, if the first half of the distribution is constrained to zero, the already poor out-of-sample forward-simulation statistics double in size; inflation is underforecast by 5 percentage points. The estimated elasticities vary between 1 and 1.5, but their 95 percent confidence intervals include unity. An interesting comparison is that the forward-simulation statistics are almost identical as between 9- and 20-quarter-lag M_2 models, even though R^2 for the 20-quarter lag is twice as large.

b. Causality Tests

M_2 is a well-known monetary aggregate, and although the M_2 monetarist inflation model cannot be correctly specified for the 1963-1971 sample period, it is important for the purposes of our study to test causality direction. Sims/Granger causality tests are made for the 1963-1976 sample periods. To be sure, these tests are incomplete, especially as regards sample homogeneity, but in view of the test results for the M_2-M_1 component described in Section 4.2c, this is not a serious omission. As before, four distributed lag regressions involving four future and eight past lags are required: past and future M_2 growth on inflation, future M_2 growth on inflation, future inflation on M_2 growth, and past and future inflation on M_2 growth. Statistically significant and relatively large-sized future lag coefficients in significant regressions of future and past lags of M_2 growth on inflation will support the null hypothesis that causality runs unidirectionally from changes in M_2 growth to changes in inflation. The summary results are presented below and provide some limited support for the null hypothesis. The asterisk denotes significance at 1 percent. The numbers inside the parentheses denote significant future lag coefficients (*t* test). The letter L or S denotes whether these coefficients are large or small relative to significant past lag coefficients. Complete estimations are presented in Tables 3A-8 and 3A-9.

For the 1963-1971 sample period both regressions involving future and past lags are significant, but not by a comfortable margin [F(4/24) = 4.2 at a 1 percent test level]. See Table 4-2. In the regression of past and future lags of M_2 growth on inflation, no future lag coefficients are significant. In the reverse regression, two future lags are significant and large-sized. The null hypothesis is supported subject to the important caveat of serially correlated residuals, absence of homogeneity tests, and estimation dependence (Almon method).

For the 1963-1976 period, only the regression of past and future M_2 growth on inflation is significant, but again not by a comfortable margin. [F(4/46) = 3.8 at a 1 percent test level]. Since no future lag coefficients were significant, there is some limited support to the null hypothesis.

Table 4-2
Sims Causality Test Summary Results for M_2

	M_2 Growth on Inflation		*Inflation on M_2 Growth*	
	Past and Future Lags	*Future Lags*	*Past and Future Lags*	*Future Lags*
F(4/24) 1963-1971	5.3*	0.9	5.3(2-3, L)*	2.5
F(4/46) 1963-1976	4.2*	0.3	1.1	0.8

Significance levels	*1 percent*	*5 percent*
F(4/24)	4.2	2.8
F(4/46)	3.8	2.6

Estimations made with Almon method, third degree polynomial. For future lag regressions, four future lags and current lag are used. For future and past lag regressions, four future, current and eight past lags are used. Complete test results in Tables 3A-8 to 3A-10.

*denotes significance at one percent test value

( ) denotes significant future lag coefficients. Letter S or L denotes relatively small or large coefficients compared to significant past lag coefficients

c. Commercial Bank Time/Savings Deposit Specification

The mildly positive Sims/Granger causality test results combined with the unsatisfactory estimation and simulation statistics for the M_2 model suggest disaggregating and testing whether its major component, M_2-M_1, is causally determinate and correctly specified in a monetarist inflation model. Disaggregating M_2 is also recommended in view of the previous economies employed in our abbreviated sensitivity analysis of the M_2 model and that time/savings deposits (M_2-M_1) comprise about two-thirds of total M_2 deposits.

The causality tests and estimations of the time/savings deposit (M_2-M_1) monetarist inflation model readily explain why the M_2 model is econometrically misspecified. The poor econometric properties of the M_2 model originate in the behavior of its major component—time/savings deposits. Sims/Granger tests indicate that time/savings deposits are causally indeterminate; hence, the mildly positive M_2 causality test results primarily reflect the strong unidirectional causality of M_1. Disaggregation, then, finds that M_2 is misspecified in monetarist inflation models on two counts—indeterminate causality of its largest component, M_2-M_1, and poor econometric results with that component.

Sensitivity Analysis. An abbreviated lag sensitivity analysis based on the 1963-1971 sample period was conducted for the M_2-M_1 model using lag

Table 4-3
Commercial Bank Time/Savings Deposit (M_2-M_1) Monetarist Inflation Model Estimations, Variable Lags, 1963-1971

	Number of Lags				
	0-9	*0-10*	*0-11*	*0-12*	*0-20*
Regression Statistics					
R^2/SE	0.31/1.42	0.31/1.43	0.30/1.43	0.34/1.39	0.43/1.29
Sum of Coefficients	−0.59	−0.70	−0.81	−0.67	0.10
(*t* value)	(−3.4)	(−3.3)	(−3.4)	(−2.7)	(0.5)
Periods with Significant Coefficients	0-1, 4-9	0-1, 5-8	0-1, 5-9	0-1, 5-9	2-6, 13-19[a]
Constant Term	9.72	11.07	12.24	10.67	Not significant
(*t* value)	(5.2)	(4.7)	(4.7)	(3.9)	
Forward Simulation Statistics					
(1971/3-1976/2)					
MAE	3.50	3.37	3.24	3.35	3.33
RMSE	4.64	4.85	5.04	4.96	4.58

[a]These coefficients are positive.

length specifications of 9 through 12 periods, and also 20 periods. The outstanding characteristics are the *negative* sum of coefficients, implausibly large positive constant term, and large forward-simulation forecast errors. The (unreliable) estimated negative sum of coefficients implies that a permanently maintained 1 percent increase in time/savings deposit growth ordinarily will be associated with a 0.7 percentage point decrease in inflation. The estimated size of the constant term is about 10. The estimated coefficients for lag periods 0, 1, and 5 to 9 remain stable, and about one-third of the variance is explained as the lag length is varied between 9 and 12 quarters. When the lag is extended to 20 quarters, R^2 rises to 0.4 although the sum of coefficients and the constant are statistically not different from zero. The statistically zero elasticity comes about because lag coefficients for periods 2 through 6 are negative and significant while lag coefficients for periods 13 through 19 are significant but positive—a curious result illustrating that R^2 is a limited statistic for purposes of evaluating distributed lag estimations.

The implausible large constant terms in the M_2-M_1 models explain the similar findings with the M_2 specification. And the out-of-sample forward simulations, underestimating inflation on the average by about 3 percentage points, readily explain the poor forward-simulation forecasts from the M_2 models. The M_2-M_1 model forward simulations predict fairly constant 3 percent inflation, beginning in 1974, quite independent of lag length specification. The estimations and simulations of the time/savings deposit (M_2-M_1) model are presented in Table 4-3.

Causality Tests. Abbreviated Sims/Granger tests were made with M_2-M_1 for the 1963-1971 and 1963-1976 sample periods. The null hypothesis is rejected, implying that the mildly positive causality test results for M_2 reflect the combined influence of strong unidirectional causality for M_1 and indeterminate causality of the larger time/savings deposit component. The summary results are presented in Table 4-4. Complete results appear in Tables 3A-7 and 3A-8.

The test cannot be applied for the 1963-1976 period; the regressions are not statistically significant. For the 1963-1971 period, the two past and future lag regressions are significant at a 1 percent testing level but not by comfortably wide margins [F(4/24) = 4.2 at 1 percent]. The two regressions involving future lags are statistically significant at a 5 percent test level, but do not have significant coefficients. In the regression of past and future time/savings deposit growth on inflation, three future lag coefficients are statistically significant. In the reverse regression, two future lag coefficients are statistically significant and relatively large-sized. The null hypothesis of unidirectional causality (in either direction) is rejected.

Table 4-4
Sims Causality Test Summary Results for M_2-M_1

	Time/Savings Deposit Growth on Inflation		*Inflation on Time/ Savings Deposit Growth*	
	Past and Future Lags	*Future Lags*	*Past and Future Lags*	*Future Lags*
F(4/24) 1963-1971	5.2 (1-3)*	3.0**	8.2 (3-4, L)*	3.3**
F(4/46) 1963-1976	0.5	0.4	0.4	0.4

Significance levels	*1 percent*	*5 percent*
F(4/24)	4.2	2.8
F(4/46)	3.8	2.6

Estimations made with Almon method, third degree polynomial. For future lag regressions, four future lags and current lag are used. For future and past lag regressions, four future, current and eight past lags are used. Complete test results in Tables 3A-8 to 3A-10.

*denotes significance at one percent test value.

**denotes significance at five percent test value.

( ) denotes significant future lag coefficients. Letter S or L denotes relatively small or large coefficients compared to significant past lag coefficients.

4.3 The M_3 Specification

It is widely recognized that time/savings deposits at commercial banks and at thrifts are close substitutes. M_3 is defined as M_2 plus time/savings deposits at thrift institutions (credit unions, mutual savings banks, and savings and loan associations) and excludes negotiable CDs exceeding $100,000. Previously M_2 had been identified as misspecified, as was its major component, time/savings deposits. Similar findings with M_3, and its time/savings deposit component, M_3-M_2, would further suggest that the monetarist inflation thesis does not apply to the broader monetary aggregates simply because the growth of interest-bearing and non-interest-bearing deposits has markedly dissimilar relationships with inflation.

a. Sensitivity Analysis

Data limitations with M_3 preclude replicating our previous procedure for making a preliminary sensitivity analysis with an arbitrarily selected 20-quarter lag where the 1956-1971 sample period was divided into two contrasting subperiods. The earliest available pre-1971 sample period for a 20-quarter-lag M_3 model begins in 1964/2. An abbreviated lag sensitivity analysis was made with lag lengths 8 to 13 for the now familiar 1963/2-1971/2 period; also the 20-quarter-lag model was estimated for the 1964/2-1971/2 period.

These estimations clearly establish that the M_3 model is misspecified. The estimated constant terms are implausibly large (11 to 19), the R^2's are low (0.2 to 0.3), and the out-of-sample forward-simulation forecasts are unusually wide of the mark. Inflation is underforecast by about 6 to 7 percentage points. An 8-quarter-lag model with five significant lag coefficients does no worse than a 12-quarter-lag with 11 significant coefficients; the additional significant lag coefficients come at the expense of doubling the already high constant terms (to a value of 18). Indeed, the 12-quarter-lag M_3 model, with 11 significant lag coefficients, nicely illustrates that significance of lag coefficients in and of itself is no indication that the model is correctly specified. The estimated M_3-price elasticities are negative and range between -1 and -2; however, their standard errors are sufficiently large so that their confidence intervals include negative unity. Also, there is clear evidence of serially correlated residuals. The estimation and simulation statistics are presented in Table 4-5.

The 20-quarter-lag M_3 model also has an implausibly large constant term, 14, and yields poor simulation forecasts, underforecasting inflation by about 5 percentage points. Interestingly, it does forecast correctly for 1976/2, demonstrating that even a misspecified model can occasionally provide a suitable forecast. By virtue of the lengthened lag, R^2 rises to 0.52; 14 coefficients are significant. The 13- and 20-quarter-lag M_3 models make for

Table 4-5

M_3 Monetarist Inflation Model Estimations, Variable Lags, 1963-1971

	Number of Lags						
	0-8	*0-9*	*0-10*	*0-11*	*0-12*	*0-13*	*0-20*[b]
Regression Statistics[a]							
R^2/SE	0.19/1.53	0.19/1.53	0.19/1.54	0.20/1.53	0.21/1.52	0.29/1.44	0.52/1.08
Sum of Coefficients (*t* value)	−1.07 (−2.98)	−1.28 (−2.70)	−1.64 (−2.66)	−2.09 (−3.04)	−1.99 (−2.81)	−1.81 (−2.68)	−1.31 (−2.25)
Periods with Significant Coefficients	0, 4-7	0-1, 4-7	0-1, 4-8	0-9	0-10	0-10, 13	4-14, 18-20[a]
Constant (*t* value)	11.34 (4.30)	12.95 (3.68)	15.66 (3.41)	18.97 (3.71)	18.24 (3.47)	17.01 (3.38)	14.02 (3.23)
Forward Simulation Statistics							
(1971/3-1976/2)							
MAE	5.74	6.23	7.03	7.75	7.70	7.34	6.13
RMSE	6.54	7.12	8.06	9.17	8.98	8.74	9.19

[a]Durbin-Watson statistics range from 0.89 for 8 lags to 1.02 for 13.

[b]Sample period begins 1964/2.

[c]These coefficients are positive.

an unusual comparison. They both have a similar number of significant lag coefficients (12 and 14, respectively) and underforecast inflation by about 5 percentage points; yet the 20-quarter-lag model has an R_2 value almost twice as large. This estimation is also presented in Table 4-5.

b. The Thrift Deposit Specification

As with M_2, the M_3 specification was disaggregated, and an abbreviated analysis was made with lag lengths 8 through 12 and 20 quarters for the thrift deposit (M_3-M_2) model. The estimations are similar to one another and are presented in Table 4-6. As expected, the sum of coefficients (M_3-M_2-price elasticity) is the same as that previously obtained with the commercial bank time/savings deposit (M_2-M_1) model, −0.7. However, the R^2 estimates are larger, about 0.6. The lag distributions have significant coefficients mostly beginning with the second previous year and continuing for a year or so. Like the M_2-M_1 models, the estimated constant terms are implausibly large, about 10 in size, suggesting that these M_3-M_2 models, too, are misspecified.

The out-of-sample forward simulations underforecast inflation by 75 percent on the average, completely missing the 1973/4 to 1975/1 surge when inflation averaged 10 percentage points. This, too, is additional evidence of misspecification.

Although elasticity estimates from the (M_2-M_1 or M_3-M_2) models are not econometrically reliable, they do have the same values, −0.7. It is clear that while a properly specified M_1 model correctly captures an econometrically reliable relationship between money growth and inflation, M_2 and M_3 do not. Apparently the relationship between the growth of

Table 4-6
Thrift Deposit (M_3-M_2) Monetarist Inflation Model Estimations, Variable Lags, 1963-1971

	Number of Lags					
	0-8	*0-9*	*0-10*	*0-11*	*0-12*	*0-20*[a]
Regression Statistics						
R^2/SE	0.56/1.13	0.55/1.14	0.55/1.14	0.58/1.11	0.60/1.08	0.55/1.04
Sum of Coefficients (*t* value)	−0.62 (−6.29)	−0.64 (−6.19)	−0.67 (−6.34)	−0.71 (−6.69)	−0.74 (−6.99)	−0.63 (−4.40)
Periods with Significant Coefficients	0, 4-7	0, 5-8	0, 5-8	1, 5-10	1, 5-11	5-16

[a]Sample period begins 1961/4 because of data limitations.

interest-earning bank deposits and inflation requires a more complicated modeling than can be provided by the single-equation monetarist inflation format.

4.4 The Reserve Aggregate Specifications

The reserve bank monetary aggregates are often considered a useful proxy for studying the effects of monetary policy and are typically used in simulation studies of large econometric models for just that purpose.[3] Most economists maintain that the Federal Reserve has good control over the reserve aggregates, if it chooses to exercise that power, for periods at least as long as a quarter of a year. The reserve and monetary aggregates are, of course, linked by the money multiplier. A study of the monetarist inflation thesis should look at several reserve aggregate specifications—total and unborrowed reserves and the reserve base. Unfortunately, data for the adjusted reserve base (reserve base adjusted for changes in reserve requirements) were not available for this study.

The reserve aggregate models were each estimated with both 10- and 15-quarter-lag specifications using the familiar 1963-1971 sample period. Additionally, out-of-sample forward simulations were made for the 10-quarter-lag models. Limited lengthening sample sensitivity tests were also made with the reserve base and nonborrowed reserve specifications. Since causality is an important issue, Sims/Granger tests were made for the promising total reserves specification. The results suggest that further work with total and nonborrowed reserve aggregates would likely yield reliable models supporting the monetarist inflation thesis.

In retrospect, it would have been more desirable to redistribute the limited resources available to this study more toward the reserve specifications. However, the strong results with M_1 were an unexpected finding, and M_1 was pursued vigorously.

a. Total Reserves

A total reserves model is approximately correctly specified with a 15-quarter uniform lag. Sims/Granger causality tests provide limited support for the hypothesized unidirectional causality.

Sensitivity Analysis. The 10-quarter-lag total reserves model has an R^2 of 0.5; and, excluding the current and last periods, the distributed lag is statistically significant with uniformly sized coefficients. The sum of coefficients (elasticity), 0.82, includes unity in its confidence interval; the constant is not significant. Increasing the lag to 15 quarters improves the R^2 by about 25 percent, to a value of 0.62. The expanded lag distribution is significant except for the first two and the last coefficients. The sum of coefficients and constant are statistically identical to those of the 10-quarter-lag model, 1 and 0, respectively. The estimations are presented in the second column of Table 4-7.

The out-of-sample forward-simulation statistics of the 10-quarter-lag total reserves model are larger than those for the 10-quarter uniformly weighted M_1 model. However, the pattern of the forecast errors is quite similar on a quarter-by-quarter comparison, overforecasting inflation until 1972, then underforecasting inflation until late 1975.

Causality Tests. Sims/Granger causality tests with total reserves provide support for the null hypothesis of unidirectional causality running from changes in total reserve growth to changes in inflation. Both regressions of past and future total reserves growth on inflation for the 1963-1971 and 1963-1976 sample periods are highly significant. For the 1963-1971 period the first two future lag coefficients are statistically significant but small-sized. They likely reflect the effects of the 8 past lag constraint inasmuch as the "true" lag coefficients are uniformly sized and the correct lag specification is about 15 quarters. In the reverse regressions involving future and past lags, relatively small-sized lag coefficients appear, but the regressions are not comfortably significant [F(4/24 = 4.2 at 1 percent test level,

Table 4-7
Reserve Aggregate Monetarist Model Estimations, 10- and 15-Quarter Lags, 1963-1971

Specification	*Reserve Base*		*Total Reserves*		*Nonborrowed Reserve*	
Number of Lag Periods	10	15	10	15	10	15
Regression Statistics						
Sum of Coefficients	2.20	1.79	0.82	0.92	0.72	0.91
(*t* value)	(6.02)	(3.09)	(5.91)	(7.31)	(5.20)	(6.16)
R^2/SE	.60/1.08	.56/1.13	.50/1.20	.62/1.05	.44/1.28	.54/1.16
Constant	−6.79	−4.51	−0.13	−0.36	0.55	−0.12
(*t* value)	(−3.85)	(−1.54)	(−0.19)	(−0.62)	(0.86)	(−0.19)
Periods with Significant Coefficients	1-10	8-13	1-9	2-14	2-10	2-14
Forward Simulation Statistics						
(1971/3-1976/2)						
RMSE	3.09	–	4.26	–	4.32	–
MAE	1.96	–	3.10	–	2.58	–

Table 4-8
Sims Causality Test Summary Results for Total Reserves

	Total Reserve Growth on Inflation		*Inflation on Total Reserve Growth*	
	Past and Future Lags	*Future Lags*	*Past and Future Lags*	*Future Lags*
F(4/24) 1963-1971	10.8 (1-2, S)*	0.7	3.2 (2-4, S)**	1.0
F(4/46) 1963-1976	13.3*	3.4**	5.5 (2-3, S)*	3.9*

Significance levels	*1 percent*	*5 percent*
F(4/24)	4.2	2.8
F(4/46)	3.8	2.6

Estimations made with Almon method, third degree polynomial. For future lag regressions, four future lags and current lag are used. For future and past lag regressions, four future, current and eight past lags are used. Complete test results in Tables 3A-8 to 3A-10.

*denotes significance at one percent test value.

**denotes significance at five percent test value.

( ) denotes significant future lag coefficients. Letter S or L denotes relatively small or large coefficients compared to significant past lag coefficients.

F(4/46) = 3.8 at 1 percent test level]. The summary results are presented in Table 4-8; complete results are found in Tables 3A-8 and 3A-9. As with the estimations of the total reserves model, these causality tests are encouraging, but having exhausted our estimation resources, we could not more intensively investigate these models.

b. Nonborrowed Reserves

The 10- and 15-quarter-lag nonborrowed reserve models are statistically identical to the total reserve models, although the R^2 is smaller. This suggests that the Sims/Granger causality test results would also be similar to those obtained for total reserves. A lengthening sample sensitivity test with the 10-quarter-lag model suggested that the lag is fairly stable and that the forward-simulation statistics are representative of the 1963/2-1971/2 sample period. In terms of forecasting ability, the simulation errors for the 1971/3-1976/2 period are only 25 percent larger than those obtained with the 10-quarter-lag uniformly weighted M_1 model.

c. Reserve Base

Since the reserve base adds public currency holdings to total reserves and we already have correctly specified the currency monetarist inflation model at 9 quarters with an elasticity of 2, we would not expect a reserve base model to be satisfactory. Recall that the total reserve model was correctly specified at approximately 15 quarters with a unit elasticity. Our expectations are confirmed.

The 10-quarter reserve base model has a significant distributed lag, except for the current period, and an R^2 of 0.6. Unlike the total and nonborrowed reserve models, the lag coefficients are not uniformly distributed but are "loaded" toward the end of the distribution. The constant term is implausibly large with a value of -6.8, and the estimated elasticity is 2.2. The out-of-sample forward simulation implausibly overforecasts inflation by about 2 percentage points but, interestingly, tracks rather accurately the 5-quarter period beginning 1973/4 when inflation averaged 10 percentage points. Lengthening sample sensitivity tests suggest that the distributed lag tail-end loading and forward-simulation forecasts are characteristic features of the 10-quarter-lag reserve base model. Lengthening the lag to 15 quarters completely changes the lag distribution. Only periods 8 to 13 retain significance, and there is a decline in performance.

The reserve base model, then, is misspecified for identifiable reasons; its currency and total reserve components have significantly different elasticities and lag lengths. We could expect that any of the variants of the reserve base adjusted for changes in reserve requirements would similarly be misspecified.

4.5 Niehans's Specification

One more money specification was briefly examined. Niehans recently suggested using the growth of the size of the Federal Reserve's government securities portfolio as a monetary policy measure.[4] For the 1963/2-1971/2 sample period, a 10-quarter-lag model with this specification gives poor results. A lengthening sample sensitivity test found no evidence of stable lag structures although most regressions were significant. Large constant terms and poor out-of-sample forward-simulation forecasts were characteristic. The best out-of-sample forward-simulation forecasts were obtained from the nonsignificant estimation for the full sample period, 1963/2-1971/2; inflation was underforecast by an average of 3 percentage points.

Notes

1. House concurrent Resolution 133, adopted in the spring of 1975, requested that the Federal Reserve set growth targets for M_1, M_2, and M_3.

2. For December 31, 1975, total deposit liabilities subject to reserve re-

quirements of all commercial banks were $506 billion, of which one-third were demand deposits. See the *Federal Reserve Bulletin*, January 1977, table 1.22, p. A15. Resource limitations precluded replication of anything like the full-scale sensitivity analysis devoted to the M_1 specification. However, estimations are not free goods, and it is more important to carefully document what appears to be a promising model rather than fully display a distressed model's embarrassment. It is unlikely that a full-scale sensitivity analysis would overturn the basic conclusions of this chapter with respect to M_2 and M_3.

3. See C. Christ, "Judging the Performance of Econometric Models of the U.S. Economy," *International Economic Review* 16, no. 1 (February 1975): 54-74; and G. Fromm and L. Klein, "A Comparison of Eleven Econometric Models of the United States," *American Economic Review* (May 1973): 385-93.

4. J. Niehans, "How to Fill an Empty Shell," *American Economic Review* (May 1976): 177-83.

5 A Forward Simulation with the M_1 Model: 1971/3-1975

5.1 Introduction and Summary

This chapter tests the second part of the monetarist inflation thesis with a 4½-year out-of-sample forward simulation of the M_1 model and closely examines the unusually interesting forecast errors. As defined in our study, the second part claims that even in the presence of unusual nonmonetary price effects, money growth remains the predominant determinant of changes in the price level. The simulation begins with the onset of wage/price controls in mid-1971 and ends two years after the oil price hike. Since we have already determined that changes in money growth satisfactorily explain inflation both before and after the simulation period (with provision for a trend factor), the forecasting errors should provide some valuable insights about the merits of competing hypotheses on the origins of inflation during the 1970s.

During the challenging period chosen to test the second part of the thesis, inflation averaged about 7 percent, more than double the 2.6 and 3.8 percent decade-average figures posted for the 1950s and 1960s, respectively; the price level increased by about one-third. And between late 1973 and late 1974 inflation nearly doubled, increasing from 7 to 12 percent. Shortly thereafter, in just one quarter, 1975/2, it dropped 5 percent, a decline unparalleled since 1951. Another feature of the simulation period is the presence of wage/price controls. Several econometric simulation studies have found that inflation was suppressed about 2 percent for the first six-quarters of controls. And we have the quadruple oil price hike in 1973/4. Finally, the period contains the sharpest recession since the 1930s. All in all, we have an interesting and varied environment in which to examine the monetarist inflation thesis. Our findings are discussed below.

Of the simulation's 18 quarters' forecasting errors, 13 are statistically significant; they appear sequentially in two separate groups with different signs. The first group of 5 quarters *overforecasts* inflation by about 2 percentage points and coincides with Phases I and II of wage/price controls. The second group of 8 quarters' forecasting errors *underforecasts* inflation by about 3.5 percentage points and closely parallels the sharp acceleration of inflation beginning with the oil price hike in 1973/4, and the subsequent deceleration in 1975. For the entire simulation period, the average absolute forecast error (MAE) is 2.3 percentage points, or about 3 times the standard error of the pre-1971 sample period. Over the period, actual and forecast inflation averaged 6.9 and 6.0 percentage points, respectively. The cumulative effect of the forecast errors is to underpredict the price level by 4 percent or less than one year's average price increase associated with the average increase in the money supply. The second part of the thesis is strongly supported.

The first group of five significant forecast errors, individually spanning the period 1971/3-1973/1, *overforecasts* inflation by 2.3 percentage points on the average, implying the existence of aggregate demand/supply effects that *suppressed* the price level below what it would have been predicted by the M_1 model. Since controls were the only unusual nonmonetary price effect that could be expected in this period to suppress price level, the forecast errors represent an indirect estimate of the price suppression effect. They are in fairly close agreement with those estimates obtained with simulations of the conventional wage/price modeling of inflation used in almost all large econometric models. The suitability of using 1971/2 as a sample endpoint is confirmed by noting that inflation is overforecast in the first simulation quarter by 1.5 percentage points, an amount absolutely larger than any of the prediction errors (residuals) for the pre-1971 sample period.

For the two quarters *separating* the first and second groups of forecast errors, 1973/2-1973/3, the simulation satisfactorily tracks inflation. The important implication is that prior to 1973/4, there is no "net foreign influence" on United States inflation. The unusual feature of the second group of forecast errors is that they closely *parallel* the movement in actual inflation between 1973/4 and 1975. In 1973/3, inflation is 7 percentage points, and the simulation is tracking correctly. Then, in the next quarter, inflation and the forecast errors each jump 2 percentage points. By 1974/4, a year after the oil price hike, they both have increased 5 percentage points. Two quarters later, in 1975/2, they both decrease 5 percentage points, and by late 1975 the simulation is again satisfactorily tracking inflation. This parallel movement suggests that excluding the overwhelming influence of money growth, the *peculiar feature* of inflation in the 1970s is the sharp 5 percentage point acceleration beginning with the oil price hike in 1973/4 and its subsequent abrupt reversal in 1975/2. During this two-year period, inflation averaged about 3.5 percentage points higher than would have been forecast by the M_1 model.

By using estimates from several econometric studies that the direct oil price hike effect on the general price level lasted about three quarters, we can infer from the forecast errors that the maximum direct oil price effect was to permanently increase the price level by about 2 percent. If the direct oil price effect was indeed limited to only three quarters, then at most only about one-third of the unusual nonmonetary increase in the price level between 1973/4 and 1975 can be attributed to a direct oil cost push pass

For 1973:4–1975:1, forecast inflation is 62% of actual. (Table 5.1)

through. However, by taking into account other suggested influences such as an expected reversal of wage/price controls, the probable direct oil price effect must have been considerably smaller, perhaps in the neighborhood of the 1 percent figure suggested by the Project Link studies.

It has been suggested that higher raw material prices are a significant causal factor behind the late-1973-1974 inflation surge. The simulation provides some valuable insights here and implies that this was not a significant factor. Casual inspection does suggest that inflation (and the forecast errors) is closely paralleled by the price cycle of various IMF dollar-denominated export price indices of nonoil primary commodities. However, by 1977 these IMF series had generally *surpassed* their earlier 1974 peaks; but when the M_1 model simulation is further extended into 1976 and 1977, the forecasts are satisfactory. Since the primary commodity price cycle is replicating itself with the simulation on track, the inference is that the earlier price cycle was not causally associated with the forecast errors between late 1973 and 1974 even though it paralleled those errors. This assessment agrees with several careful input/output studies that find only a very small cost push pass through on the general price level from higher primary commodity prices.

It is clear that the M_1 model cannot be patched up with the addition of one or more variables for purposes of econometrically "explaining" the 1973-1975 forecast errors, at least not with any confidence in the results. A single-equation model is simply too clumsy a tool for explaining the complicated interactions during this unusual 9-quarter period. For example, it is difficult to understand how the nonoil "net foreign influence" proxied by primary commodity or import prices could be reliably estimated in an extended single-equation M_1 model. Changes in aggregate demand induced by money growth is itself a major determinant of primary commodity prices! Also, prices of primary commodities are influenced by the demand for the United States dollar in international currency markets which in turn is strongly influenced by United States inflation. The interactions between the foreign influence, on the one hand, and inflation and money growth, on the other, are certainly complex and not unidirectional. A more complicated modelling than can be provided by an extended M_1 model is required.

The author's view is that the 5-quarter inflation surge beginning in 1973/4 and the subsequent collapse reflect primarily the peculiar circumstance in which the oil shock occurred. The oil price hike in 1973/4 was imposed upon an economy that had been expanding for two years and was about to begin to reverse the significant suppression of prices achieved by the controls. (The simulation clearly suggests the price suppression ended in 1973/1, but the reversal did not yet begin in the next two quarters.) Since the economy was about to begin a significant upward price adjustment as a natural consequence of relaxing controls, and since output was expanding,

— the oil shock generated an expectations-augmented surge in excess demand with materials stockpiling/hoarding. After a year of declining real output, it was clear that the excess demand was unsupportable; expectations and excess demand abruptly collapsed in 1975/2, by which time the controls' price adjustment reversal had been completed, as was the oil hike cost push pass through.

An attractive feature of this explanation is that the same forces that explain the surge in inflation *also* explain the sudden decline in inflation in 1975/2. The unwinding of the controls' price suppression effects works in only one direction and would have been completed by early 1975. The oil price hike cost push pass through upon the price structure could be expected to have been completed by early 1975. And a sudden collapse in excess demand could not have been expected to depress the price level below what would have been predicted by the M_1 model.

Note that money growth, which played such a dominant role in determining the price level during the simulation period, together with the unwinding of the controls' suppression effects would be sufficient to account for almost 9 percent inflation during the 5-quarter acceleration period, not too far removed from the 10.5 percent average inflation for that period. Allowing 1 to 1.5 percent for the direct oil cost push pass through, then at the 1974/4 inflation peak of 12 percent, the contribution from excess demand need only be in the range of 2 to 2.5 percentage points. This is not an unreasonable figure for a powerful shock imposed upon an expanding economy beginning to undertake a major price adjustment in response to earlier wage/price controls. Thus, the monetarist framework for explaining inflation also provides a plausible explanation for the unusual behavior of the price level between late 1973 and 1975.

Summing up, during the 4½-year simulation, the price level rose by about 33 percent with all but 4 percent predicted by the M_1 model. The second part of the monetarist inflation thesis is strongly supported. Moreover, the forecast errors are unusually suggestive. The first group implies a 2 percent price level suppression effect, agreeing with the assessment from econometric studies of controls. And the second group closely parallels the surge in inflation beginning in 1973/4 and the abrupt decline in 1975. The forecast errors suggest no significant nonoil "foreign influence," a modest role for oil cost push pass through, and a significant role for the reversal of the controls' suppression effect. It appears that the peculiar timing of the oil price hike, imposed upon an expanding economy about to begin a major price adjustment in response to earlier wage/price controls, largely explains the dramatic rise in the price level in 1974. While this suggestive explanation fits into the monetarist framework, it cannot be buttressed by an econometric extension of the single-equation M_1 model. The model is far too clumsy for such purposes. All in all, the simulation not only supports the thesis, but provides some highly suggestive insights.

The organization of this chapter is as follows. A brief statistical overview of the forecast errors is provided in the Section 5.2. Then in Section 5.3, the second part of the monetarist inflation thesis is tested with the simulation's forecast errors. Finally, in Section 5.4, we closely examine at some length the forecast errors. Attention is given to the findings from other studies of inflation in this period and also the formidable econometric problems involved in extending the M_1 model to account for unusual non-monetary effects on the price level.

5.2 An Overview of the Simulation

In this section we briefly review the unusually interesting set of forecast errors from the out-of-sample forward simulation of the M_1 model. They are presented in Table 5-1. Recall from Chapter 3 that prior to the simulation,

Table 5-1
Forecast Inflation, Actual Inflation, and Forecasting Errors, 1971/3-1975/4

Period	*(1) Actual Inflation*	*(2) Forecast Inflation*	*(3) = (2) – (1) Forecast Errors*
1971/3	3.3%	4.8%	1.5%*
4	3.5	4.3	0.8
1972/1	5.6	4.7	–0.9
2	2.8	5.4	2.6*
3	3.4	6.2	2.8*
4	4.6	6.9	2.3*
1973/1	5.7	7.2	1.5*
2	6.8	7.3	0.5
3	7.3	7.4	0.1
4	9.2	7.2	–2.0*
1974/1	9.1	6.7	–2.4*
2	10.9	6.5	–4.4*
3	11.0	6.7	–4.3*
4	11.9	6.3	–5.6*
1975/1	10.3	5.4	–4.9*
2	5.6	5.2	0.4
3	7.1	4.9	–2.2*
4	6.1	4.3	–1.8*
Mean	6.9	6.0	–0.9

MAE is 2.3 percent.

*denotes forecast errors exceeding 2 standard errors, 1.6 percent.

pre-1971/2, inflation was satisfactorily explained by the M_1 model; when the simulation was extended into 1976 and 1977, the inflation forecasts were also satisfactory. On the whole, in the simulation period, inflation is underforecast by about 2 percentage points, but the forecast errors are sequentially bunched into two separate groups with different signs. The first group of five statistically significant forecast errors *overforecasts* inflation and coincides with Phases I and II of wage/price controls at the beginning of the simulation. The second group of eight significant forecast errors *underforecasts* inflation and closely parallels the sharp acceleration of inflation beginning with the quadruple oil hike in 1973/4 and subsequent abrupt deceleration in 1975/2.

Owing to the sign reversal between the two groups of significant forecast errors, inflation is underforecast on the average by about 1 percentage point for the entire simulation period; actual and forecast inflation are 6.9 and 6.0 percentage points, respectively. However, the mean absolute error (MAE) is 2.3 percentage points, or about 3 times the M_1 model's standard error for the 1963-1971 sample period, 0.81 percentage points. Of the 18 simulation quarters, 11 quarters have forecast errors that are clearly significant by the usual convention that they exceed 2 standard errors, 1.6. Two others are sufficiently close (1.5 percentage points) that they, too, deserve to be considered significant. Since the forecast errors in 13 quarters or about three-fourths of the simulation are statistically significant, the implication is that while the M_1 model satisfactorily explains inflation both before 1971/2 and after 1975/4, there are unusual nonmonetary factors to be accounted for in the in-between period.

The first group of five significant errors, beginning with the onset of wage/price controls and spanning the period 1971/3-1973/1, represents an *overforecast* of inflation by an average of 2.1 percentage points, implying that conditions in the economy caused inflation to be lower (suppressed) than would have been predicted on the basis of the M_1 model. This is not an unexpected finding since four of the errors coincide with the first 6 quarters of Phases I and II of controls. We do have important econometric evidence from other studies that wage/price controls had a significant suppression effect of about 2 percentage points for the first 6 quarters of controls (see Section 5.4a). In retrospect, the onset of controls was a suitably chosen sample endpoint. Inflation is overforecast in the first quarter of the simulation, 1971/3, by 1.5 percentage points, an amount in absolute size exceeding the prediction error (residual) of any quarter the pre-1971/2 sample period. Recall that the residual in the last quarter of the sample period was zero and that the residuals averaged out (to zero) in each of the last three preceding years of the sample period. On casual inspection, then, the first 6 quarters of the simulation do not have any unexpected surprises.

Certainly the most interesting part of the simulation is the second group of eight forecast errors that closely parallel the sharp acceleration and abrupt deceleration of inflation between 1973/4 and the end of 1975. Over this two-year period, inflation is underforecast by about 3 percentage points. For half a year preceding this forecast error sequence inflation averaged about 7 percent and the simulation was on target, with an average forecast error of only 0.3 percentage point. Then in 1973/4, the quarter in which the quadruple oil price hike occurred, inflation and the forecast errors *both* jumped 2 percentage points. One year later, 1974/4, they had *both* increased by 5 percentage points over their 1973/3 values as inflation peaked at about 12 percent. Two quarters later, 1975/2, they *both* dropped 5 percentage points, and by the end of 1975 the simulation is satisfactorily forecasting inflation.

5.3 Does the Monetary Influence Predominate?

The second part of the monetarist inflation thesis (as defined in this study) claims that money growth will remain the major determinant of inflation even in the presence of unusual nonmonetary price effects. The 18-quarter forward simulation of the 10-quarter-lag uniformly weighted M_1 model, previously identified in Chapter 3 as reliable for the 1956-1971 sample period, provides an opportunity to test the second part of the thesis. Predominance can be assessed in two ways. On a quarter-by-quarter basis, we can simply compare the magnitudes of forecast inflation with the forecast errors representing unusual nonmonetary inflation. If, for each quarter, forecast inflation is larger than the forecast error, then the monetary influence on inflation is considered size-predominant. This would be a strong result. Second, the forecast period can be assessed as a whole. If the unusual nonmonetary price effects are only a temporary phenomenon, then their lasting influence should be a permanent rise in the price level rather than a source of continuing inflation. This would imply that the model in effect "survives" unusual nonmonetary influences on the price level. To make this comparison, two price indices need be computed. The 18-quarter series of forecast inflation is forward-cumulated into a price index of predicted inflation, beginning in 1971/3. Similarly, the actual quarterly inflation figures are also forward-cumulated into a price index with the same starting date, 1971/3. By approximately late 1975, the index of predicted inflation should be below the index of actual inflation. If the two series remain statistically parallel after this date, then we have evidence that the lasting influence of the unusual nonmonetary price effects was only a permanent rise in the price level. Furthermore, if the difference between the two series, representing the permanent induced rise in the price level by 4½ years of cumulative unusual nonmonetary price effects, is less than one year's average increase in the price level predicted by the M_1 model for the simulation period, about 6 percent, then we have clear evidence that money growth was the predominant continuing source of inflation.

Looking at Table 5-1, we find that in each of the 18 quarters, predicted inflation exceeds in absolute size the forecast errors, representing unusual nonmonetary inflation. Even when only the 13 quarters with statistically significant forecast errors are considered, their mean absolute error of 2.9 percentage points is only about one-half the average size of predicted inflation. For the period as a whole, forecast inflation averaged 6.0 percentage points, and actual inflation averaged 6.9 percentage points. In only four quarters, 1974/2-1975/1, do the forecast errors (averaging 4.8 percentage points) begin to approach the size of predicted inflation (averaging 6.2 percentage points). The evidence, then, suggests that money growth remained the primary source of inflation in the simulation period, and together with the trend factor was responsible for about 6 percent averge inflation. More accurately, the effects on the price level from changes in aggregate demand were sufficiently well captured by the M_1 model in the simulation period that unusual aggregate demand/supply price effects were not the dominant influence.

The two price indices by which the simulation period as a whole can be examined are presented in Table 5-2. Beginning late 1975, the two series remain statistically *parallel* by about 4 percentage points, suggesting that unusual nonmonetary price effects permanently raised the price level by 4 percent, or less than one year's average increase generated by M_1 growth during the simulation period. The M_1 model, in effect, survives the significant but not overwhelming presence of unusual nonmonetary price effects. The major determinant of inflation during the simulation period was M_1 growth.

5.4 A Closer Look at the Forecast Errors

While the second part of the monetarist inflation thesis is clearly supported by the 4½-year forward simulation, and extending the simulation into 1976 and 1977 satisfactorily forecasts inflation, the forecast errors do need to be explained. Potentially, they are a rich source of information. Any study that depends in part on the results of a forward simulation is obligated to explain significant forecast errors or at least explain why it is difficult (or impossible) to do so within the analytical framework adopted in that study. We begin this section by using noneconometric methods to obtain conditional inferences from the forecast errors about two specific "events" that occurred during the simulation period: wage/price controls and the OPEC-inspired quadruple oil price hike. In making these inferences, we use findings from other studies. Then, we focus in the unusually interesting second

Table 5-2
Actual and Predicted Cumulative Price Indices, 1971/3-1976/4

Period	*Index of Actual Prices*	*Index of Forecast Prices*	*Difference Expressed in Annual Growth Rates*
1971/3	96.53	96.89	−0.4%
4	97.38	97.83	−0.5
1972/1	98.76	99.08	−0.3
2	99.45	100.43	−1.0
3	100.29	101.98	−1.7
4	101.44	103.75	−2.3
1973/1	102.89	105.62	−2.7
2	104.65	107.56	−2.8
3	106.57	109.54	−2.8
4	109.05	111.50	−2.9
1974/1	111.28	113.36	−1.9
2	114.34	115.20	−0.8
3	117.52	117.13	0.3
4	121.06	118.97	1.7
1975/1	124.21	120.57	2.9
2	125.96	122.13	3.0
3	128.20	123.65	3.6
4	130.17	124.97	4.0
1976/1	131.47	126.18	4.0
2	133.06	127.52	4.2
3	134.56	128.83	4.3
4	136.35	130.17	4.5

Actual price index refers to implicit GNP deflator. Forecast price index refers to prices predicted by the forward simulation of the 10-quarter-lag uniformly weighted M_1 Model.

$$\text{Column 3} = \frac{\text{Column 2}}{\text{Column 1}} - 1$$

group of forecast errors and discuss to what extent they can be explained by a "net foreign influence." The inherent econometric problems of extending the M_1 model to explain the net foreign influence on inflation are briefly discussed. Finally, a qualified interpretation of the forecasting errors is offered.

To be sure, there is no shortage of explanations for the unparalleled late-1973-1975 surge in peacetime inflation in the United States and other industrialized economies.[1] Indeed, the number of explanations is almost as large as the number of observations in our simulation period! On many lists would be shortfalls in agricultural production (especially in the Soviet Union), coincidence of strong synchronized aggregate demand among the industrialized economies, OPEC-inspired quadruple oil price hike, sharp export price increases in primary commodities, dollar devaluation, adoption of floating exchange rates, and increase in world money supply. Since a major component of the industrialized economies' currencies forming the "world money supply" construct is the United States dollar, and since the M_1 model yields relatively modest forecast errors for the post-1971/2 period, by inference from our study we must look beyond world money growth.

a. Controls

Unlike all the other unusual nonmonetary price effects usually suggested as relevant for the post-1971/2 period, wage/price controls are the only suggested influence that would be expected to *suppress* the price level. Moreover, the initial effects are easily dated—August 1971. And econometric studies of controls suggest they were moderately effective in suppressing inflation at least until late 1972, coinciding with the end of Phase II.[2]

Our hypothesis is that for the first 6 quarters of controls, corresponding to Phases I and II, wage/price controls were the *dominant* unusual nonmonetary price effect. The hypothesis is conditional on the reasonable assumption that controls were the only unusual nonmonetary influence that could be expected to suppress prices. It is also important to note that the "true" suppression effects of controls would be visible only if controls were the only unusual nonmonetary price effect during this period. However, the 2 percentage point jump in the GNP deflator and CPI index during 1972/1 is acknowledged to have originated in food prices.[3] The full controls' suppression effect would be expected to be submerged in that period. To support the hypothesis, the forecast errors should overforecast inflation by statistically significant amounts for most of the 6 quarters, excluding 1972/1.

Examining the first six forecast errors in Table 5-1, we observe that five have the correct sign and four are statistically significant with a mean value of 2.1 percentage points. The cumulative overforecast by late 1972 is 2.3 percentage points (see Table 5-2). Excluding the "food inflation" quarter, 1972/1, the forecast errors average 2.0 percentage points and support the conditional hypothesis that controls were the dominant unusual nonmonetary price effect from 1971/3 to 1972/4. The similarity between the cumulative forecast error and estimates obtained from simulations with wage/price econometric models suggests that a closer comparison is warranted. Fortunately, the Pierce-Enzler controls simulation of the MIT-Penn-SSRC (MPS) model provides estimates for each of the 6 quarters.[4] Two caveats should be mentioned. The Pierce-Enzler study uses the consumer products (CP) implicit price deflator, and the M_1 model's estimates of controls' effects are *impure* inasmuch as they include the net combined effects of a controls suppression together with other influences working to increase the price level. The M_1 model controls simulation is indirect since other effects may be included, but inasmuch as they would be of opposite sign, the forecast errors can be understood as a controls simulation; i.e. the true controls effect would be at least as large as the forecast errors. The comparisons are shown in Table 5-3.

The two series are reasonably similar. Both have the sign reversal in 1972/1 (the food inflation quarter); the most pronounced difference is the Pierce-Enzler estimate of a 4.1 percentage point suppression effect in 1971/4. However, the food inflation bulge between November and February undoubtedly masks the "true" controls effect suggested by the M_1 model forecast error. Excluding this quarter, the M_1 and Pierce-Enzler simulations suggest that the average suppression effect was 1.7 and 1.8 percentage points, respectively. The difference between these figures is well within the difference between the implicit CP and GNP deflators. All in all, excluding 1971/4, the M_1 forecast errors are in close agreement with the Pierce-Enzler controls simulation. It is not often that similar simulations are obtained from quite different modeling approaches.

b. The Oil Price Hike

Some conditional inferences about the direct price effects of the quadruple oil price hike cost push pass through on the general price level can be made from the forecast errors. The oil hike occurred in two steps—from \$3 to \$5.13 per barrel in October 1973, and a further increase to \$11.65 in

Table 5-3
Comparative Controls Simulations, 1971/3-1972/4

Period	*Inflation (GNP Deflator)*	*M_1 Model Simulation*	*Inflation (CP Deflator)*	*Pierce-Enzler Controls Simulation*
1971/3	3.3%	1.5%	4.6%	1.6%
4	3.5	0.8	2.5	4.1
1972/1	5.6	−0.9	4.5	−0.6
2	2.8	2.6	2.4	3.1
3	3.4	2.8	3.2	3.0
4	4.6	2.3	3.6	1.8
Mean	3.9	1.5	3.5	2.2

December. From other studies we have estimates that the direct oil price effects lasted about three quarters. Also, we know that prior to the price hike, the simulation was satisfactorily forecasting inflation. On the other hand, any inferences about oil from the three-quarter period, 1973/4-1974/2, need be couched in terms of maximum effects since it is reasonable to suppose that the controls suppression effect was unwinding at this time. And there were probably other unusual nonmonetary influences affecting the price level in addition to oil and the controls' suppression reversal. With these caveats, the forecast errors have some interesting insights about the direct oil price effects.

To fix the length of time over which the direct oil price effect lasted for purposes of making inferences from the forecast errors, we rely on estimates from two econometric simulation studies. The Pierce-Enzler oil effect simulation study with the large MPS econometric model of the United States economy and the Gordon simulation with a conventional two-equation wage/price econometric model both suggest a 3-quarter oil price effect.[5] Additional evidence comes from an unpublished Department of Commerce unit value index of imported fuels. This index reported sharp jumps for three successive quarters beginning in 1973/4 with the major jump in 1974/1.[6] Prior to 1973/4 and after 1974/2, this index remained stable. Together these findings suggest that insofar as the forecast errors have a direct oil price component, our attention should be focused on the first three quarters of the second group of forecast errors, 1973/4-1974/2.

From Table 5-1 we observe that the forecast errors for this period are 2.0, 2.4, and 4.4 percentage points, respectively. Their 2.9 percent average is roughly in line with the Pierce-Enzler and Gordon estimates of 3.3 and 2.6 percent, respectively. However, the third quarter's error, 4.4 percentage points, is too large. The Pierce-Enzler study suggests a more sensible declining sequence of 4.2 (9.7), 3.1 (11.6), and 2.5 (11.6) percentage points, respectively, where the consumer products implicit price deflator figures used to measure inflation appear in parentheses. By arbitrarily cutting the third quarter's forecast error in half, the average error is reduced to about 2.2 percentage points. Since the simulation underforecasts for five additional quarters, it is clear that if the direct oil effect was limited to three quarters, then it could not be the major unusual nonmonetary price effect between late 1973 and 1975.

Once the maximum direct oil price effect has been estimated, we need to work downward from that figure. It is reasonable to suppose that the controls' price suppression effects were subsequently reversed. Indeed, looking at Table 5-2, we observe that if the reversal begins in 1973/4, none of the forecast errors prior to 1974/3 need be attributed to oil! Now, it is outside the province of this study to allocate the forecast errors between oil and the unwinding of the controls' suppression effect, but it is reasonable to suppose that the unwinding began in late 1973 or soon after and was completed perhaps within a year. Additionally, a further dilution of the forecast error's maximum oil contribution can be made with reference to a foreign influence by way of higher primary commodity prices, and perhaps changes in aggregate domestic demand not captured by money growth. The point, however, is that at most, the three quarters' oil price effect implied by the forecast errors is a permanent price level rise of about 1.7 percent. But it is almost certain that in accounting for controls' suppression unwinding, if not other influences, the implied oil effect was well below that figure, more in line with the very modest assessment by the Project Link controls' simulation of less than 1 percent.[7]

c. *The Net Foreign Influence*

Prior to the quadruple oil price hike quarter, 1973/4, inflation is satisfactorily explained (sensibly allowing for a wage/price controls' suppression effect) within the general framework used in this study—changes in the general price level are determined by changes in aggregate demand induced by changes in the monetary impulse. But beginning 1973/4, the sharp *parallel* acceleration in both the forecast errors and inflation itself does not fit into an aggregate framework as conventionally measured. The price acceleration began in that quarter designated by the NBER as the cyclical peak and *continued* for an additional four quarters despite negative real growth throughout that year and the next. Real GNP declined at about a 2 percent rate during 1974-1975. Ordinarily, the upward pressure on the general price level associated with expansions in economic activity as capacity constraints and bottlenecks develop tends to be reversed once the cyclical peak is passed. It is true, however, that this dampening effect on prices has become progressively weaker in the postwar period.[8] The question, then, is why the monetarist aggregate demand framework used in this study for explaining inflation should be satisfactory both prior to 1973/4 and after late 1975 but, on casual inspection, does not appear to be satisfactory for the intervening two-year period.

One way of preserving the aggregate demand framework is to appeal to a foreign influence, i.e. imported inflation. The unusual synchronized expansion of economic activity in 1972-1973 among the industrialized economies falls into this category. For example, real output among the OECD economies grew 8 percent in 1973, outpacing the United States average of 5.5 percent in 1972-1973.[9] It is also true that the subsequent contraction in economic activity was *also* synchronized. Industrial production among the OECD countries declined 10 percent in 1975; real output in the United States declined 2 percent during 1974-1975.[10] Yet when we examine the forecast errors in 1975, we do not find *any* evidence that forecast inflation was above actual inflation. There is no inference that any of the previous increase in the price level that might have been attributed to the synchronized expansion was reversed during the synchronized contraction. Unless the industrialized economies have a ratchet mechanism where synchronized activity can only increase prices but not work in the reverse direction, the forecast errors suggest that the source of the unusual increase in the price level was not the synchronized expansion of economic activity.

In search of a foreign influence on the United States price level, we can also look at the cost side, such as higher prices of primary commodities or more generally higher prices on imports. For example, the world export minerals price index, which averaged 118 between 1963 and 1971, registered a whopping 477 in 1974. The problem of tracking down the "net" foreign influence is obviously complicated because the cost push is not immediate but involves successive rounds of production, some of the imported price increase was reexported, all prices didn't increase proportionally, and higher prices inevitably affect the composition and level of aggregate demand.

In a recent article, Louis Goreau presents 15 indices of market prices (denominated in dollars) of nonoil primary commodities exported by producing countries that were prepared by the IMF.[11] We find that their weighted index peaks in 1974/2, some three quarters past the United States cyclical peak, and bottoms out in 1975/2, roughly coincident with the recession trough. With only two exceptions, the indices of the individual commodities peaked within plus or minus two quarters of the weighted peak for all commodities. About the trough, there was more dispersion. Goreau also constructs an index of *real* primary commodities, defined as the ratio of nonoil primary commodities divided by an index of manufactured export product prices. This index, too, also peaks in 1974/2 and bottoms in 1975/2. Now, the interesting feature of these indices prepared by the IMF is that they match very nicely the forecast errors of the M_1 model simulation! If one were looking for an additional variable to add to the M_1 model to explain the 1973-1975 errors, the weighted IMF primary commodity export price series would do nicely indeed.

However, when the IMF series are extended, this unusual "happy coincidence" can be turned around. The primary commodity IMF series generally *regain* their former peaks (1974/2) by early 1977, but while their price cycle is replicating itself, there was no similar surge in inflation at home or abroad.[12] Indeed, the M_1 model simulation, when extended further into 1976 and 1977, forecasts rather nicely. The inference is that if the primary commodity price cycle is replicating itself again and tracks an earlier set of forecast errors but isn't needed to match the second set, then it is reasonable to maintain that they were not a significant causal determinant of 1974-1975 nonmonetary inflation. Highly aggregated models that "explain" the 1974-1975 inflation surge by significant reference to import prices appear to be misspecified.[13]

d. Expanding the M_1 Model to Capture the Net Foreign Influence

Since this is an econometric study, it is worthwhile to consider the prospects of expanding the highly aggregated M_1 model to explain the net foreign influence. It is clear that a dummy variable can easily capture the earlier price effects from wage/price controls, but a noneconometric approach did nicely, too. First, let us examine the prospects for an expansion with an exogenous foreign-effects variable. To test causality, a Sims/Granger test is appropriate; but since the test involves the use of distributed lag time-series regressions and there are at most eight relevant foreign price effect quarters, for all practical purposes exogeneity cannot be tested.

There are some serious difficulties in estimating the coefficient of a foreign-effects variable. Conceptually, the foreign-effects variable must be interrelated with money growth. After all, changes in money growth induce changes in aggregate demand, which in turn is an important determinant of prices of primary commodities and imported goods. The United States is a "big engine" in foreign trade. And since the United States dollar has a conspicuously important role in foreign currency markets and foreign trade generally, its fortunes in the foreign currency market will also influence primary commodity prices. Thus, not only is a foreign price effects variable influenced by money growth, but it is clearly not unidirectionally causal with respect to inflation.

Since the variance-covariance matrix between money growth and the foreign price effects variable is nonzero, the obvious test for whether the foreign price effects variable is correctly specified is if the money growth distributed lag coefficients remain unchanged when the sample period is extended through 1977 as the primary commodity price cycle is replicating itself.[14] Foreign effects are needed (perhaps) in 1974-1975 but not in 1976-1977! And a lag is almost certainly involved, but with only eight relevant foreign-effects quarters, it cannot be specified with any confidence. A careful sensitivity test is out of the question. And then we need to account for the oil price hike and the reversal of wage/price controls' suppression effect. Without beating a dead horse, the M_1 model clearly cannot be expanded to econometrically "explain" the unusual behavior of the price level between late 1973 and 1975. A highly aggregated single-equation model is too clumsy for that delicate and demanding task. For serious econometric insights we need access to input/output and/or multiequation models to unravel that period.

5.5 A Suggested Explanation of the 1973/4-1974 Inflation Surge

While it is clear that there "is no percentage" in expanding the M_1 model for purposes of econometrically explaining the late-1973-1974 inflation surge, the forecast errors do provide sufficient insights for an unusually simple explanation that fits comfortably within the monetarist aggregate demand approach. It is offered as a monetarist explanation with extreme simplicity as one of its virtues (hopefully not the only one).

The origins of the late-1973 inflation surge primarily reflect the peculiar setting in which the quadruple oil price hike was imposed. The economy had been expanding at a sustained basis for two years and was about to begin a major price adjustment, reversing the controls' suppresion effects. Recall that the simulation clearly indicates that the reversal could not have begun prior to 1973/4; it was tracking correctly for half a year prior to the oil price hike. This insight is of particular importance because the unwinding of the controls' suppression effect when added to the M_1 model's forecast would have together accounted for almost 9 percent inflation during the surge period, not far removed from the actual 10.5 percent figure.

With the inevitable major price adjustment waiting in the wings (controls could hardly be expected to permanently depress the price level), the oil shock imposed upon an expanding economy induced a surge in *excess demand* accompanied by sharp upward price expectations and raw materials stockpiling and general goods hoarding. Perhaps a suspicion that controls might be reinstituted was just below the surface, too. After a year had passed and it was clear that there was no underlying sustaining increase in real aggregate demand, excess demand collapsed. An attractive feature of appealing to an expectations-based excess demand explanation is that it offers a plausible explanation of the precipitous drop in inflation (and the forecast errors) in 1975/2, and squares with the important observation that in 1975 actual inflation never was less than predicted inflation. The controls reversal was probably completed in four or five quarters and was no longer a source of upward pressure on the price level. Similarly, the direct cost push pass through from the oil price hike apparently lasted no more than three or four quarters. And a collapse in excess demand would not be expected to depress the price level below the level reflecting continuing changes in aggregate demand generated by money growth.

In this interpretation, only three factors are required to explain the 5 percent inflation surge and the subsequent deceleration: controls reversal, direct oil cost push pass through, and expectations-based excess demand. The timing of the oil price hike was perfect, although that was surely unforeseen. Guess-estimating, the 4 percent permanent increase in the price level gets allocated as follows: 1 to 1.5 percent for the direct oil cost push pass through; about 2 percent for expectations-based excess demand; and perhaps 0.5 percent for a foreign influence. If this suggested explanation is near the mark, then by inference the reaction to the oil price shock would have been substantially smaller had the economy not been poised for a major price and wage adjustment following the relaxation of controls. The crucial insight from the simulation, then, is that the controls reversal did not start prior to the oil price hike quarter.

A final note. That the simulation comes back on track by late 1975 suggests a remarkable stability of the dynamic price adjustment process. It also supports the basic framework used in this study to explain changes in the price level by changes in aggregate demand induced by the monetary impulse. One surprise is the absence of any visible output price effect near the recession trough, but perhaps that effect is masked by the apparent collapse in excess demand in early 1975. It will be interesting to see how the simulation tracks during the next recession; an overforecast would imply such an output effect on the price level. The author's guess is that as long as money growth remains at uncharacteristically high rates, the effects from changes in output and velocity upon the price level will be overshadowed by the powerful, stable money growth-inflation relationship.

Notes

1. A representative sampling, and only a sampling, of the burgeoning literature is as follows: For input-output studies of the cost push effect of foreign price increases, see Cagan (1977) and Berner et al. (1975). Both studies attribute not more than 20 percent of the above trend 1973-1974 price increase to the cost push of foreign influences. For aggregate demand single-equation studies employing foreign price indices to represent foreign influences, see Weintraub (1976) and Keran and Riordin (1976). These less sophisticated studies suggest foreign price effects very much larger than those suggested by the input/output studies above. On food effects see Schnittker (1973) and Hathaway (1974). On oil effects see the Pierce-Enzler (1974) simulation of the MPS econometric model, Gordon (1975), and the Project Link studies (1976) directed by Larry Klein. On wages see Nordhaus (1972). Also see Kaldor (1976) and the Parkin and Zis (1974) and the Meiselman and Laffer (1975) volumes. Finally Fieleke (1976) in a wide-ranging article suggests that Germany, heavily dependent on foreign trade and supposedly less insulated than the United States from primary commodity export price increases, maintained a relatively low inflation in the 1973-1975 period, implying that there is more to explaining the inflation surge than simply cost push from higher commodity prices.

Staff Report of the Subcommittee on Domestic Monetary Policy of the

Committee on Banking, Currency and Housing, House of Representatives, *The Impact of the Federal Reserve Systems Monetary Policies on the Nation's Economy*, 94th Cong., 2d Sess., December 1976, prepared by R. Weintraub; M. Keran and M. Riordin, "Stabilization Policy in a World Context," *Economic Review* of the Federal Reserve Bank of San Francisco, Fall 1976, pp. 5-19; J. Schnittker, "The 1972-73 Food Price Spiral," *BPEA* 2 (1973):498-506; D. Hathaway, "Food Prices and Inflation," *BPEA* 1 (1974):63-109; W. Nordhaus, "The Worldwide Wage Explosion," *BPEA* 2 (1972):431-64; N. Kaldor, "Inflation and Recession in the World Economy," *The Economic Journal* 86 (December 1976):703-14; Manchester Conference Papers on Inflation in the World Economy, published in M. Parkin and G. Zis (eds.), *Inflation in the World Economy* (University of Toronto Press, 1974); D. Meiselman and A. Laffer (eds.) *The Phenomenon of Worldwide Inflation* (Washington: American Enterprise Institute for Public Policy Research, 1975); R. Berner, P. Clark, J. Enzler, and B. Lowrey, "International Sources of Domestic Inflation," Joint Economic Committee *Studies in Price Stability and Economic Growth*, Paper No. 3 in International Aspects of Recent Inflation, 94th Cong., 1st Sess., August 1975; P. Cagan, *The Effect of World Prices on U.S. Inflation* (NBER, 1977) multilith; N. Fieleke, "The Worldwide Inflation," *New England Economic Review*, Federal Reserve Bank of Boston, May/June 1976; J. Pierce and J. Enzler, "The Effects of External Inflationary Shocks," *BPEA* 1 (1974):13-54; R. Gordon, "The Impact of Demand on Prices," *BPEA* 3 (1975):613-62.

2. Estimates of the price suppression effect from the first six quarters of controls range from little effect to about two percentage points. The Council of Economic Advisors, in their 1973 and 1974 *Annual Reports*, did not view controls as a major constraining influence. They noted that only half of all wages and prices were subject to controls, and important sectors of the economy such as raw agricultural commodities, imports, and exports were exempted. Cagan (1973) maintains that controls appeared to work in 1972 because of slack demand associated with the recession. Kosters (1975) finds little evidence of a controls effect. See also Bosworth (1972) and Mitchell (1974).

The econometric evaluation of controls' effectiveness suggest a 2 percent suppression effect until late 1972. See the Pierce-Enzler (1974) simulation of controls with the large MPS econometric model. Gordon has made a continuing series of studies using the conventional wage/price econometric model format and also suggests that controls had about a 2 percentage point suppression effect on inflation.

P. Cagan, "Controls and Monetary Policy, 1969-1971," in *A New Look at Inflation* (Washington: American Enterprise Institute, 1973), pp.

1-34; M. Kosters, *Controls and Inflation* (Washington: American Enterprise Institute, 1975); B. Bosworth, "Phase II: The U.S. Experiment with an Incomes Policy," *BPEA* 2 (1972): 343-83; D. Mitchell, "Phase II Wage Controls," *Industrial and Labor Relations Review* 27 (April 1974): 351-75; J. Pierce and J. Enzler, "The Effects of External Inflationary Shocks," *BPEA* 1 (1974): 13-54; R. Gordon, "Can the Inflation of the 1970's Be Explained?" *BPEA* 1 (1977): 253-76; R. Gordon, "The Impact of Aggregate Demand on Prices," *BPEA* 3 (1975): 613-62; R. Gordon, "The Response of Wages and Prices to the First Two Years of Controls," *BPEA* 2 (1973): 765-78; R. Gordon, "Wage/Price Controls and the Shifting Phillips Curve," *BPEA* 2 (1972): 385-421.

3. *Annual Report of the Council of Economic Advisors*, 1973, p. 57. Farm commodity prices in 1972 registered their sharpest gains since World War I. A representative listing of the boost in food prices is as follows:

	1963-1971 Average	*1972*	*1973*
World export foodstuffs price index	105	132	191
WPI farm product component increase	2%	14%	27%
CPI food component increase	3%	5%	20%

Schnittker (p. 502) argues that the agricultural price increase reflects "The strong demand for meat, poor 1972 harvests, and a pervasive world wide inability to expand the output of protein meals enough to stabilize prices. . . ." J. Schnittker, "The 1972-73 Food Price Spiral," *BPEA* 2 (1973):498-506. He also notes (p. 501) that the sharp rise in meat prices in 1973 ". . . represents the acceleration of an established trend, not a new development. World beef prices doubled from 1963-71. . ."

4. Pierce and Enzler, "Effects of External Inflationary Shocks."

5. Pierce and Enzler, "Effects of External Inflationary Shocks," and Gordon, "Impact of Aggregate Demand on Prices." The Pierce-Enzler study reported the results of seven simulations of the large MPS econometric model of the United States economy using different sets of assumptions. The first year's price effects ranged between 2.5 and 2.8 percentage points on an annual basis, using the CP deflator, with virtually all the effects coming in the first three quarters. The average oil effect for three quarters was an additional 3.3 percentage points inflation.

6. Supplied courtesy of Jonathan C. Menes, Director of the Applied Research Division, U.S. Department of Commerce.

7. J. Waelbroeck (ed.), *The Models of Project Link* (North Holland, 1976).

8. P. Cagan, *The Hydra Headed Monster: The Problem of Inflation in the United States* (Washington: American Enterprise Institute, 1974).

9. N. Kaldor, "Inflation and Recession in the World Economy," *The Economic Journal* 86 (December 1976):703-14.

10. Ibid.

11. L.M. Goreau, "The Use of Compensatory Financing," *Finance and Development* 14, no. 3 (September 1977): 20-24.

12. Ibid.

13. For example, Weintraub, using a single-equation approach, implausibly estimates that foreign prices raised the CPI by about 5.5 percentage points in 1974! Staff Report of the Subcommittee on Domestic Monetary Policy of the Committee on Banking, Currency and Housing, House of Representatives, *The Impact of the Federal Reserve Systems Monetary Policies on the Nation's Economy*, 94th Cong., 2nd Sess., 1976, prepared by R. Weintraub.

14. None of the single-equation highly aggregated studies, e.g. Weintraub, that have come to the author's attention make this obvious test which should be sufficient to point out the unsuitability of the approach. In the Weintraub study, extending the sample period to 1977 would be sufficient for the test to show that the import price variable was misspecified.

6 The M_1 Model's Inflation Implications for Monetary Policy

6.1 Introduction and Summary

The M_1 monetarist inflation model has important implications about the proper conduct of monetary policy with respect to inflation. In this chapter we discuss the long-run values of inflation associated with various M_1 growth trends, forecast inflation out to 1980, propose an anti-inflation money growth policy, and suggest quarterly M_1 growth rate guidelines for purposes of stabilizing inflation. The first inquiry involves the static equilibrium solutions of the M_1 model; the second and fourth require out-of-sample forward simulations. The policy prescription suggests that a phased reduction of M_1 growth would require 4 to 5 years to make serious inroads against inflation and would inevitably conflict with the Federal Reserve's conventional countercyclical monetary policy pursuits.

The static equilibrium solution of the M_1 model implies that constant 2 percent M_1 growth would yield complete price stability, i.e. no change in the implicit GNP price deflator. Three percent M_1 growth would yield about 1.5 percent inflation. Tying M_1 growth to the average postwar real GNP gain of about 4 percent would yield 3 percent inflation, moderate with respect to the 1970s but not with respect to the 1950s. The M_1 model implies that by posting M_1 growth targets, the Federal Reserve, in effect, publicly announces its inflation policy. With targets of 4 to 6.5 percent, the implied range of inflation is between 3 and 6.5 percent. However, last year's (1977) 7 percent M_1 growth average implies a trend inflation of 7 percent. The inflation implied by constant or trend M_1 growth is readily computed by multiplying the desired M_1 growth by 1.4 (the M_1-price elasticity) and then adding the constant, -2.7.

Comparing the M_1 model's price stability requirements of 2 percent M_1 growth with the conventional prescription suggests that perhaps 2 percent is a magic number as regards inflation. Conventional markup over labor cost models ordinarily explain inflation without any explicit reference to money growth; current-dollar wage cost increases in excess of labor trend productivity gain, roughly 2 percent per annum, are considered inflationary.

The forward simulations with the M_1 model, beginning in 1978/1, suggest that if the Federal Reserve maintains last year's 7 percent M_1 growth rate, inflation will rise to 7 percent by late 1978 and to almost 8 percent in 1979. If the economy receives less monetary stimulus in 1978, say 5 or 6 percent M_1 growth, inflation will continue at 1977's pace of 6 percent. Even if last year's 7 percent M_1 growth rate were cut in half for 1978, inflation would still average better than 5 percent. These forecasts are not surprising since the M_1 model incorporates a uniformly weighted lag over 2½ years and the full impact of last year's 7 percent M_1 growth will be felt in 1978 and 1979. Finally, it is worth noting that if the money spigot is opened up, several years of 8 or 9 percent M_1 growth will bring us just below double-digit inflation.

These gloomy inflation forecasts suggest that there are few, if any, prospects for reducing inflation unless there is a planned reduction in M_1 growth. The real question is how to move from last year's 7 percent money growth to somewhere in the neighborhood of the 2 percent figure associated with stable prices. Broadly speaking, two approaches are available—"biting the bullet" with an immediate adoption of 2 percent money growth, or a gradual money growth reduction by a fixed amount, say 1 or 1.5 percent per annum. The first approach would require about 2½ years, but there would be little immediately visible progress. Inflation would average 5 percent in the first year but would be below 3 percent by the end of the second year. A more gradual money growth reduction, say 1 percent per annum, would require 4 to 5 years to achieve price stability; there would be no visible progress from such a policy during the first two years. On the other hand, a gradual reduction formula would minimize any product and/or labor market adjustment problems (real or imagined) and avoid a temporary credit crunch.

Since 1980 is an election year and we are into a mature phase of the current economic recovery at the time of writing (January 1978), the present prospects for adopting the above anti-inflationary money growth program are not promising. From a longer perspective a central difficulty is that the number of years required to achieve price stability through a phased money growth reduction is fairly long relative to the average business cycle expansion. The postwar exception is the expansion of the 1960s, but that was fueled in part by excessive money growth. It may be a decade or more before our "independent" Federal Reserve substantially lowers money growth rates.

A congressional mandate to achieve price stability would require a program of preset annual M_1 growth targets for at least 4 or 5 years. During this time, countercyclical monetary policy would be held in abeyance with due regard for unforeseen contingencies. Not only would we have a real opportunity to see if the M_1 model works as well in reverse, but we could also assess whether the private sector would enjoy greater stability from a carefully regulated monetary impulse.

In the last topic discussed in this chapter, forward simulations with M_1 growth cycles about preselected growth trends provide some guidelines on how much variability in quarterly M_1 growth rates can be tolerated without significantly departing from a desired inflation figure. These simulations suggest that once a desired M_1 growth trend is selected, no constraints on quarterly M_1 growth needs be imposed other than requiring that M_1 growth averages out to the trend value every four quarters. Even absolutely large quarterly M_1 growth rate deviations from a preselected trend will have little effect on quarterly inflation figures. On the other hand, if the averaging takes place over a period as long as eight quarters, then even relatively small quarterly M_1 growth rate deviations from the preselected trend can induce substantial changes in quarterly inflation figures. These findings suggest that if we are interested in monitoring whether quarterly M_1 growth rates are deviating from a preselected trend, we need to observe the 4-quarter sequence of money growth rates.

The organization of the chapter is as follows. In Section 6.2, the static equilibrium inflation-money growth solutions of the M_1 model are discussed. Inflation forecasts out to 1980 under a broad spectrum of alternative future M_1 growth paths are presented in Section 6.3. The strategies of reducing M_1 growth to a rate consistent with price stability are discussed in detail in Section 6.4. Finally, in Section 6.5, forward simulations are used to suggest some guidelines as to how much variability in quarterly M_1 growth rates about a given M_1 growth trend can be accepted before significantly affecting quarterly inflation figures.

6.2 Inflation Associated with M_1 Growth Trends

In this section we discuss the M_1 model's equilibrium inflation values associated with long-run or trend money growth, especially as regards the requirements for a stable price level. These static equilibrium solutions of the 10-quarter uniformly weighted lag M_1 model are readily obtained by multiplying the M_1 price elasticity, 1.4, by the desired M_1 growth trend and then adding to this figure the constant term, −2.7. Some representative tabulations are as follows:

Trend M_1 Growth	*Inflation*
2%	0%
3	1.6
4	3.0
5	4.4
6	5.9
8	8.5
10	11.5

These figures suggest that complete price stability, i.e. no growth in the implicit GNP price deflator, requires 2 percent M_1 growth. Moderate price stability (in terms of the experience of the 1970s but not that of the 1950s), say 2.5 percent inflation, requires 3.5 percent M_1 growth. Tying M_1 growth to the average postwar real GNP gain of about 4 percent per annum would yield 3 percent inflation. The Federal Reserve's target ranges for M_1 growth, 4 to 6.5 percent, imply 3 to 6.5 percent inflation. Indeed, the Federal Reserve, simply by posting M_1 growth targets, in effect publicly announces its inflation policy. Since it is widely held that the economy presently has a "built in" inflation "momentum" of about 6 percent, it is noteworthy that the M_1 model's implied inflation from the 6 percent average M_1 growth of the 1970s is also 6 percent. Last year (1977) even more stimulus was added to the economy; M_1 growth averaged 7 percent. Maintaining 7 percent M_1 growth implies 7 percent inflation. Unless M_1 growth is substantially reduced, there are, according to the M_1 model, few, if any, prospects for significantly lowering inflation. Strategies for reducing M_1 growth will be discussed in Section 6.4.

The above static equilibrium solutions of the M_1 model can also be couched in terms of velocity growth. Using the familiar equation of exchange expressed as an identity in growth rates ($m + v = p + q$) and assuming that real output (q) grows at its approximate potential of about 4 percent, we have the following figures:

p	m	v ($q = 4\%$)
0%	2%	2%
3	4	3
6	6	4
8.5	8	4.5

At approximately full employment output growth, say 3 to 4 percent per annum, price stability would be accompanied by a small increase in velocity, about 1 to 2 percent per annum. Over the 20-year period we have studied, velocity has almost doubled its mid-1950 value of about 3, implying a growth rate of about 3 percent per annum. By implication, a sizable portion of that growth has been associated by the unusual growth in the narrow money stock.

Implications from the static equilibrium conditions of the M_1 model are, of course, based on its continued stability. We have seen that the M_1-price elasticity, incorporating the direct effects of the monetary impulse on the price level, has been impressively stable for the last 20 years. And the constant term has been stable for about 15 years. In the future, the model may again shift, but given the uniformly weighted lag extending over 2½ years, we would be forewarned by increasingly poor inflation forecasts. If the early 1960s downward shift is wholly or partially reversed, price stability will require even lower money growth. However, given the continued stability of the M_1-price elasticity during the 1970s, we can have reasonable confidence that low money growth, say 2 percent per annum, is the prescription for a stable price level in the foreseeable future.

In concluding this section, it is useful to compare the M_1 model's price stability requirements with those suggested by conventional wage/price econometric modeling. As noted in Section 5.4a, empirically that approach focuses primarily on the excess of current-dollar labor cost increase over labor trend productivity gain, roughly 2 to 3 percent per annum, and secondarily upon measures of demand (supply) pressures in the goods and labor markets. The usual finding is that the wage/price elasticity is 1, where wages are defined as current-dollar labor costs in excess of labor trend productivity gain. The implication is that wage gains exceeding 2 to 3 percent per annum are inflationary. Thus, the conventional approach, focusing directly on the goods and labor markets and not explicitly recognizing M_1 growth as a causal variable, implies that price stability requires wage gains be held to about 2 percent per annum. And the M_1 monetarist inflation approach, not explicitly recognizing demand (supply) effects in the goods and labor markets, implies that M_1 growth be held to about 2 percent. Perhaps 2 percent is a magic number as regards price stability. If both approaches are valid, the obvious task is to combine them in a more complex modeling; but it is not clear how to do this. Most economists would feel uncomfortable about explaining inflation without explicit reference to demand (supply) pressures in the goods and labor markets. Similarly, others would be uncomfortable about not explicitly recognizing the role of money growth. To its credit, the money growth approach is supported by evidence suggesting that causality is unidirectional, running from changes in money growth to changes in inflation.

6.3 Post-1978 Inflation Forecasts

In this section the 10-quarter uniformly weighted lag M_1 model is used to forecast inflation beginning in 1978/1. The forecasts are made in the usual fashion, multiplying the sum of the current and 10 previous quarters of M_1 growth by the uniform weight, 0.13, and then adding to that product the constant term, -2.7. After 10 quarters have elapsed (1980/3), the influence of pre-1978/1 actual M_1 growth rates is lost and the static equilibrium solutions apply, as discussed in Section 6.2. In order to make these forecasts, future M_1 growth paths need to be projected. Forecasts based on a variety of constant M_1 growth rates are presented in Table 6-1. Note that the

Table 6-1
Post-1978 Inflation Forecasts with the M_1 Model

	Inflation Implied at Various Constant M_1 Growth Rates (%)								
Period	*2*	*3*	*4*	*5*	*6*	*7*	*8*	*9*	*10*
1978/1	5.4	5.5	5.6	5.8	5.9	6.0	6.2	6.3	6.4
2	4.7	5.0	5.3	5.2	5.8	6.0	6.3	6.6	6.8
3	4.7	5.1	5.5	5.9	6.2	6.6	7.0	7.4	7.8
4	4.6	5.1	5.6	6.1	6.4	7.2	7.7	8.2	8.7
1979/1	3.8	4.4	5.1	5.7	6.4	7.0	7.7	8.3	9.0
2	3.5	4.2	5.0	5.8	6.6	7.4	8.1	8.9	9.7
3	2.0	3.8	4.7	5.6	6.5	7.4	8.4	9.3	10.2
4	2.6	3.6	4.7	5.7	6.8	7.8	8.8	9.9	10.9
1980/1	1.8	2.9	4.1	5.3	6.5	7.6	8.8	10.0	11.1
2	0.8	2.1	3.4	4.7	6.0	7.3	8.6	9.9	11.2
3	0.2	1.6	3.1	4.5	5.9	7.3	8.8	10.2	11.6
4	0.2	1.6	3.1	4.5	5.9	7.3	8.8	10.2	11.6

By 1980/3 the influence of pre-1978 M_1 growth rates has been lost and no longer influences the 10-quarter uniformly distributed lag.

forecasts are made in terms of constant M_1 growth rates but would be little changed if M_1 growth varies from quarter to quarter (as it would in practice) as long as the quarterly growth rates average out to the values in the table over the course of four quarters.

Inspection of Table 6-1 suggests that if the Federal Reserve continues last year's 7 percent M_1 growth, inflation will rise to 7 percent by the end of 1978. With even more stimulus this year, say 8 percent M_1 growth, inflation will nudge the 8 percent mark. Two additional years of 7 percent M_1 growth will bring 8 percent inflation. Several years of 8 percent M_1 growth will bring us within range of double-digit inflation. These forecasts are not surprising, since by virtue of the 2½-year uniformly weighted lag, the full impact of 1977's M_1 growth will continue to be felt in 1978 and 1979. On the other hand, if the Federal Reserve reverses gears and reduces M_1 growth to 5 or 6 percent in 1978, inflation would continue at its current 6 percent pace. Even a year of inspired 4 percent M_1 growth would yield only a modest dividend; inflation would average 5.5 percent.

6.4 An Anti-Inflation Money Growth Policy

These gloomy inflation forecasts together with the creditable out-of-sample forecasting record for 1976-1977 suggest that unless there is a planned reduction in M_1 growth, there are little, if any, prospects for reducing inflation. Given last year's 7 percent M_1 growth and the two percent M_1 growth requirements for complete price stability, the real question is what strategy to propose for lowering M_1 growth. Broadly speaking, we have two options—"biting the bullet" immediately with a 2 percent M_1 growth diet, and a more gradual approach, reducing M_1 growth by a fixed amount over several years. Since adoption of 2 percent M_1 growth would probably precipitate a "credit crunch" and may have some short-run temporary effects on the product and labor markets, it is not likely that such a policy would be adopted; but the projection path does provide some insights on the *minimum* time required to achieve stable prices.

The projected inflation path from biting the bullet with 2 percent M_1 growth beginning in 1978/1 is presented in the left-hand column of Table 6-1. In the first year (1978), there would be little visible progress; inflation would average 5 percentage points. In the second year (1979), inflation would average just over 3 percentage points and would be below 3 percentage points by the year's end. Midway into the third year, the goal of price stability would be realized. About 2 to 2½ years, then, is the minimum time required to achieve price stability under a crash program. Thus, quite independent of any adjustment problems (real or imagined) which are not considered here, it is clear that inflation is not subject to a quick fix.

To examine the gradual approach of progressively lowering M_1 growth by a constant rate each year, three projections, beginning in 1978/1, were made with 1, 1.5, and 2 percent annual reduction formulas. Under the 1 percent annual reduction rule, M_1 growth would average 6 percent in 1978 (down 1 percent from 1977's rate), then average 5 percent in 1979, and so on. Under the 2 percent annual reduction rule, M_1 growth would average 5 percent in 1978, then 3 percent in 1979, and so on. The projections are based in terms of constant M_1 growth for each year but would be essentially unchanged if M_1 growth varied from quarter to quarter (as it would in practice) so long as it averaged each year to the constant growth rate used in the projections. By virtue of the 2½-year uniformly weighted lag, the projections are not handicapped by assuming constant M_1 growth rates. While there are differing views on the Federal Reserve's ability to control quarterly M_1 growth rates, few would have any serious reservations on its ability to control M_1 growth on an annual basis.

From the three projections of inflation presented in Table 6-2 we observe that price stability requires about 5 years under a 1 percent yearly growth reduction rule, 3½ years under a 1.5 percent rule, and 2½ years under a 2 percent rule. Note that there would be *no visible progress* during the first year under any of these three rules. Indeed, under the 1 percent rule, progress would be painfully slow. Inflation would remain unchanged at 6 percent for the first two years and would average only 5 percent in the

Table 6-2
Inflation Forecasts under Annual M_1 Growth Reduction Proposals

	1 Percent Reduction per Year		*1.5 Percent Reduction per Year*		*2 Percent Reduction per Year*	
	M_1 Growth	*Inflation*	*M_1 Growth*	*Inflation*	*M_1 Growth*	*Inflation*
1978/1		5.9%		5.8%		5.8%
2	6%	5.8	55%	5.7	5%	5.5
3		6.2		6.0		5.9
4		6.6		6.4		6.1
1979/1		6.2		5.8		5.5
2	5	6.3	4	5.8	3	5.3
3		6.1		5.5		4.8
4		6.2		5.5		4.7
1980/1		5.7		4.7		3.7
2	4	5.0	2.5	3.8	1	2.7
3		4.6		3.2		1.9
4		4.4		2.9		1.4
1981/1		4.0		2.3		
2	3	3.6	1	1.7		
3		3.2		1.1		
4		2.9		0.7		
1982/1		2.5				
2	2	2.1				
3		1.8				
4		1.5				

the third year. Even under the 2 percent annual reduction rule, inflation would average 5 percent in the second year.

The considerable time that would be required to make serious inroads against inflation under a sustained program of gradually reducing money growth by, say, 1 percent per annum makes the adoption of such a program unlikely in the near future. To follow that program requires that the Federal Reserve temporarily abandon its traditional pursuit of countercyclical monetary policy. At the time of this writing (January 1978), we are well into a mature phase of the economic recovery from the March 1975 recession trough. Since 1980 is an election year, there would be little visible progress in reducing inflation; yet perhaps there would be some real prospects of a recession, at least based on the average of postwar business cycles. Ideally, the program outlined above should be pursued during a sustained economic expansion such as we experienced during the 1960s. Since that expansion was fueled in part by strong money growth, we may have to wait a decade or more before an "independent" but politically attuned Federal Reserve could complete a money growth reduction program.

The anti-inflation program outlined above requires a major departure in the conduct of monetary policy as practiced by the Federal Reserve since it regained its independence in the early 1950s. If the Federal Reserve were required by Congress to control M_1 growth in terms of preset declining yearly averages for purposes of reducing inflation, such a policy would be far more constraining than the current posting of targets in accord with House Concurrent Resolution 133 (spring 1975). The reference dates for those targets have been changed by the Federal Reserve, and 1977's M_1 growth rate of 7 percent exceeded the "official" target upper range of 6.5 percent. What is required to achieve a measure of price stability within 4 to 5 years is no less than the temporary abandonment of discretionary countercyclical monetary policy. While it is not the purview of this study to assess the real or imagined output and employment "costs" of following a gradual sustained reduction in money growth over half a decade, such a program would be an enormously interesting economic experiment. We would learn whether a stabilized (but gradually lowered) M_1 growth rate would, in fact, remove a major source of instability from the private sector, as is often claimed by monetarist economists.[1] It would also be interesting to observe credit market behavior under such a program. The Federal Reserve, of course, would still have considerable short-term flexibility with respect to M_1 growth. If the money growth reduction proposal was successful in that the price level was stabilized and the private sector showed increased stability without tending toward recession, then we might want to consider additional constraints on the Federal Reserve's ability to conduct discretionary countercyclical monetary policy. Thus the M_1 model implies that a determined attempt to return to the halcyon days of fairly stable prices requires a major rethinking of the proper conduct of monetary policy in the United States.

6.5 Variability of M_1 Growth and Stability of Inflation

While the amount of M_1 outstanding has almost always increased from one quarter to the next in the postwar period, it has done so at varying growth rates. For example, between 1963 and 1976, the standard deviation of quarterly M_1 growth was 2.3 percentage points, or almost one-half the mean growth rate. The higher M_1 growth characteristic of the 1970s has been accompanied by relatively less quarter-to-quarter variation. The standard deviation of M_1 growth was 2.3 percent for both the 1963-1971 and

1971-1976 periods, implying that with higher average M_1 growth, the coefficient of variation declined over time. Since it is neither technically feasible nor desirable to maintain perfectly constant quarterly M_1 growth rates, it is important to know how much variation can be tolerated before significantly affecting a desired inflation figure. A series of simulation experiments with the M_1 monetarist inflation model suggests some useful guidelines.

a. Constructing M_1 Growth Cycles

In principle, there are an infinite number of ways of generating variations or cycles of M_1 growth about a desired trend rate or narrow band. Once several representative M_1 growth trends are selected, the major concern is creating a representative group of simple M_1 growth variation sequences or cycles about each of several preselected trends. To keep things fairly manageable while exploring the possibilities, three M_1 growth *trends* (4, 5, and 6 percent) and three variation *sequences* (3, 4, and 8 quarters long, respectively) together with two M_1 growth *deviations* from the trend (2 and 4 percentage points, respectively) are selected. This procedure generates 18 different M_1 growth paths (three growth trends × two deviation amounts × three variation sequences). These cycles by no means provide a definitive assessment, but they do cover a broad range of possibilities.

The three variation sequences or cycles of M_1 growth about each M_1 growth trend are as follows.

(1) The first sequence is a *three-quarter* pattern with a quarter's M_1 growth above the trend rate, then a quarter's growth at the trend rate, and finally a quarter's growth below the trend rate. Over three quarters, M_1 growth averages to the trend rate. For example, with a 4 percent M_1 growth trend and a 2 percentage point deviation from trend, the quarterly sequence of M_1 growth rates (in percent) becomes 6, 4, 2, 6, 4, 2, and so on. With a 4 percentage point deviation from trend, the sequence now becomes (in percent) 8, 4, 0, 8, 4, 0, ... Similar sequences are readily generated about the other two M_1 growth trends. The six possible M_1 growth cycles or sequences, each three quarters long, are presented in the left-hand column of Table 6-3.

(2) The second sequence is a *four-quarter* long pattern with two quarters of M_1 growth above the trend, then two quarters below the trend. Over four quarters, M_1 growth averages to the trend. For example, with a 4 percent trend and a 2 percentage point deviation from the trend, the quarterly sequence of M_1 growth becomes (in percent) 6, 6, 2, 2, 6, 6, 2, 2, ... The six possible growth sequences, each four quarters long, are presented in middle column of Table 6-3.

(3) The third sequence is an *eight-quarter* pattern with four quarters of M_1 growth above the trend and then four quarters below the trend. Over eight

Table 6-3
Cycles in M_1 Growth about Selected Trend Rates

M_1 Growth Trend Rate (%)	Deviation in M_1 Growth from Trend Rate (%)	Cyclical M_1 Growth Rates (%) 3-Quarter Cycle	4-Quarter Cycle	8-Quarter Cycle
4	2	6, 4, 2, . . .	6, 6, 2, 2, . . .	6, 6, 6, 6, 2, 2, 2, 2, . . .
	4	8, 4, 0, . . .	8, 8, 0, 0, . . .	8, 8, 8, 8, 0, 0, 0, 0, . . .
5	2	7, 5, 3, . . .	7, 7, 3, 3, . . .	7, 7, 7, 7, 3, 3, 3, 3, . . .
	4	9, 5, 1, . . .	9, 9, 1, 1, . . .	9, 9, 9, 9, 1, 1, 1, 1, . . .
6	2	8, 6, 4, . . .	8, 8, 4, 4, . . .	8, 8, 8, 8, 4, 4, 4, 4, . . .
	4	10, 6, 2, . . .	10, 10, 2, 2, . . .	10, 10, 10, 10, 2, 2, 2, 2, . . .

quarters, M_1 growth averages to the trend. For example, with a 4 percent M_1 growth trend and a 2 percentage point deviation from trend, the sequence becomes (in percent) 6, 6, 6, 6, 2, 2, 2, 2, 6, 6, 6, 6, 2, 2, 2, 2, ... The six possible M_1 growth sequences, each eight quarters long, are presented in the right-hand column of Table 6-3.

Note that the deviations from the trend rates, 2 and 4 percentage points, are disproportionate to the size of the trend rates. The deviations are 50 and 100 percent of the 4 percent M_1 trend rate but only 33 and 66 percent of the 6 percent M_1 trend rate.

b. The Simulated Inflation Paths

The 18 simulated inflation paths generated by the M_1 growth cycles are presented in three figures. Figure 6-1 presents six simulations of inflation corresponding to variations in M_1 growth about the 4 percent M_1 growth trend. Similarly, inflation generated by variations about the 5 percent M_1 growth trend is presented in Figure 6-2, and inflation generated by variations about the 6 percent M_1 growth trend is presented in Figure 6-3. Each projected inflation path fluctuates about the static equilibrium inflation value appropriate to that particular M_1 growth trend (see Section 6.2). For the 4 percent M_1 growth trend, the static equilibrium inflation value (Figure 6-1) is 3 percent. The respective static equilibrium inflation values are 4.4 percent for the 5 percent M_1 growth trend (Figure 6-2) and 5.8 percent for the 6 percent M_1 growth trend (Figure 6-3). Each simulation begins in 1976/3 and continues for 23 quarters.[2] The influence of actual pre-1976/3 M_1 growth rates is lost after 11 quarters.

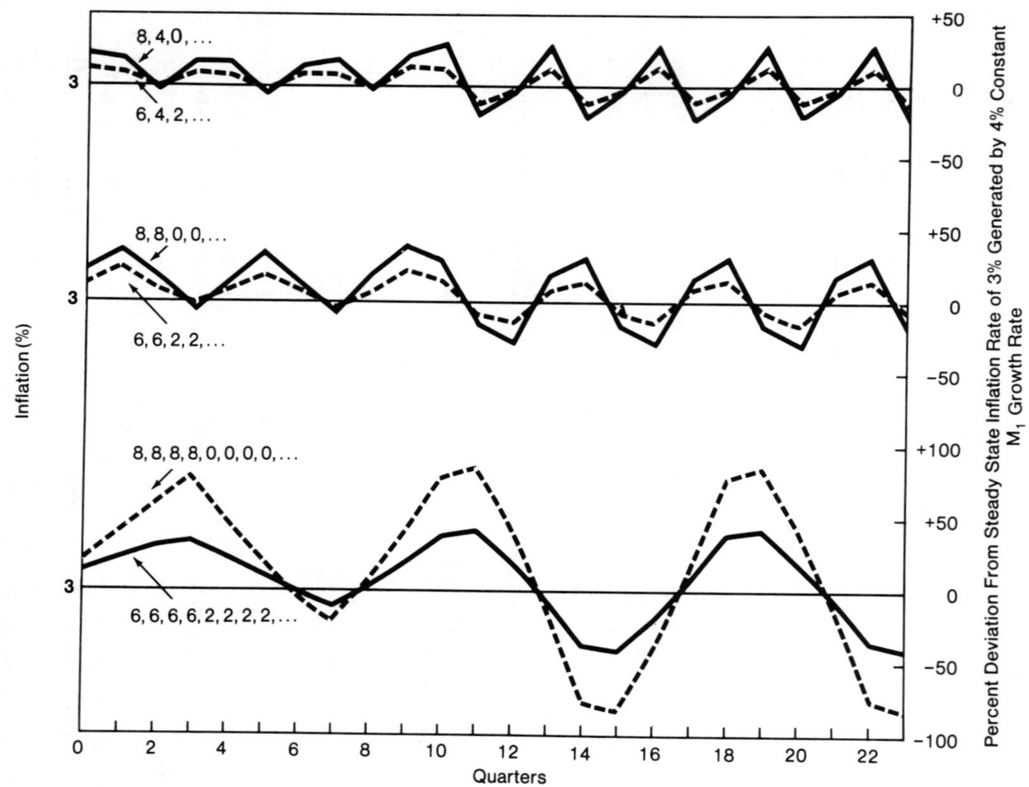

Figure 6-1. Simulated Inflation from Cycles in M_1 Growth about a 4 Percent Trend

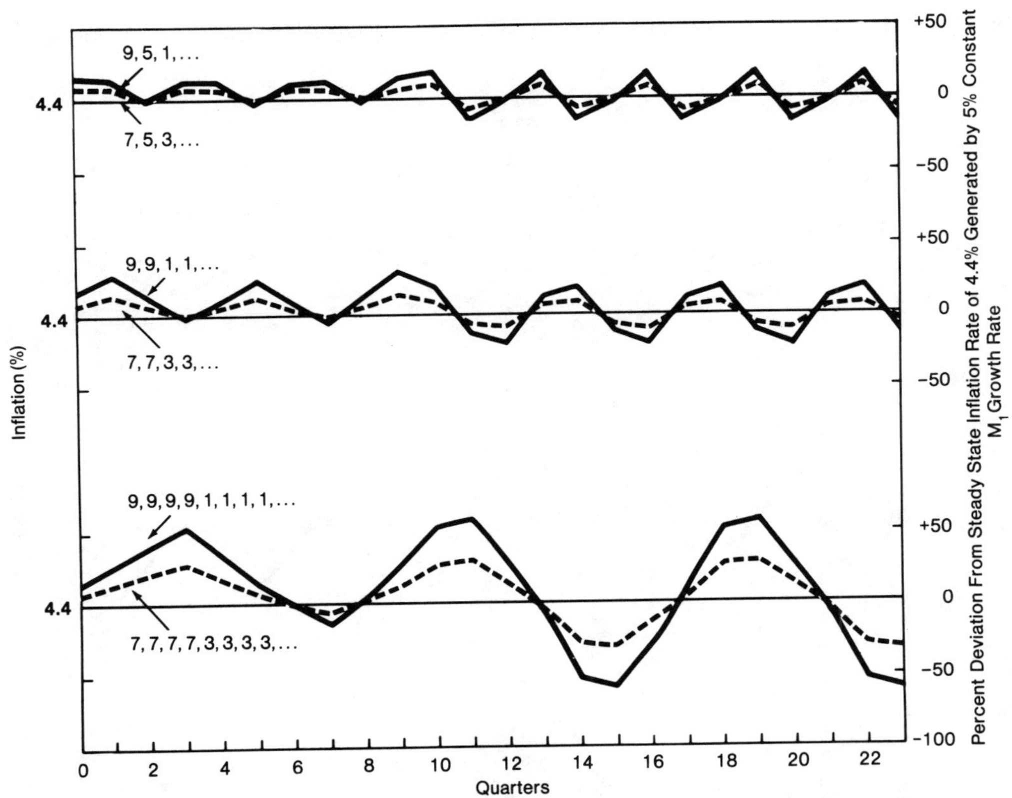

Figure 6-2. Simulated Inflation from Cycles in M_1 Growth about a 5 Percent Trend

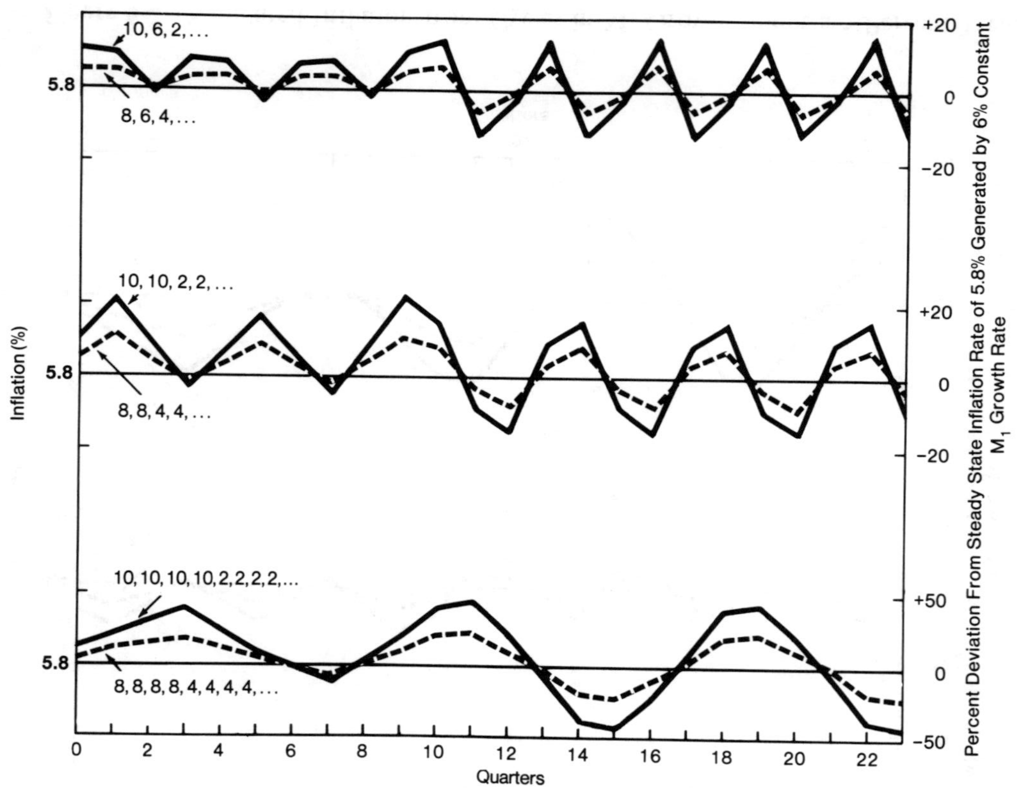

Figure 6-3. Simulated Inflation from Cycles in M_1 Growth about a 6 Percent Trend

Inspecting the six simulations generated from varying M_1 growth about the 4 percent M_1 growth trend in Figure 6-1, it is clear that the *time interval* over which the averaging sequence takes place is the *dominant factor*, not the amount of deviation in M_1 growth from its trend. For the three- and four-quarter cycles, the maximum impact on inflation from variations in M_1 growth about the 4 percent M_1 trend is only 0.75 percentage point. But for an 8-quarter sequence, the maximum effect is quite large, 2.6 percentage points; for this sequence, observed inflation ranges in value from 0.4 to 5.6 percentage points. Even if M_1 growth varies by only 2 percentage points about the 4 percent trend over an 8-quarter cycle, inflation ranges in value between 1.8 to 4.2 percentage points. The implication is clear. Relatively large deviations in M_1 growth about a desired trend have little effect on current inflation as long as the deviations average out over 3 to 4 quarters. But with a longer averaging sequence, say two years, relatively small M_1 deviations from the trend can substantially affect current inflation. Similar implications follow from studying inflation simulations from cycles about the 5 percent M_1 growth trend (Figure 6-2) and the 6 percent M_1 growth trend (Figure 6-3).

The simulations suggest that for purposes of stabilizing inflation, it would be preferable to require that the Federal Reserve average out M_1 growth rates to a specified trend value within about 4 quarters rather than the current practice of setting broad target ranges. William Poole has suggested on general grounds that the Federal Reserve should adopt a money stock growth trend together with an allowable (percentage) band of deviation.[3] However, for purposes of stabilizing inflation, it is the *time* over which the averaging takes place, rather than the permissible deviation from the money growth trend, that warrants attention. If the Federal Reserve is required or chooses to average out M_1 growth within a year or so, then for purposes of stabilizing inflation, we do not need be concerned about permissible ranges or percentage deviations from trend.

Notes

1. See Thomas Mayer, "The Structure of Monetarism," in *Kredit and Kapital* 1(April 1975): 204.

2. The simulations begın in 1976/3 simply because the estimation of the M_1 model was completed in that quarter.

3. See William Poole, "Interpreting the Fed's Monetary Targets," *BPEA* 1(1976): 257.

Bibliography

Almon, Shirley. "The Distributed Lag between Capital Appropriations and Expenditures." *Econometrica* 33 (1965): 178-96.

Andersen, Leonall, and Denis Karnosky. "The Appropriate Time Frame for Controlling Monetary Aggregates: The St. Louis Evidence." In *Controlling Monetary Aggregates II: The Implementation.* Conference Series No. 9 (Federal Reserve Bank of Boston), September 1972, pp. 147-77.

Berner, Richard, Peter Clark, Jared Enzler, and Barbara Lowrey. "International Sources of Domestic Inflation." Joint Economic Committee *Studies in Price Stability and Economic Growth.* Paper 3 in International Aspects of Recent Inflation. 94th Cong., 1st Sess., August 1975.

Bosworth, Barry. "Phase II: The U.S. Experiment with an Incomes Policy." *BPEA* 2(1972): 343-83.

Brunner, Karl. "The Role of Money and Monetary Policy." *Review* (Federal Reserve Bank of St. Louis), July 1968, pp. 8-24.

Brunner, Karl, and Allan Meltzer. "Money, Debt and Economic Activity." *Journal of Political Economy* 80, no. 5 (September/October 1972): 951-77.

Burger, A., and D. Mudd. "The FOMC in 1976: Progress against Inflation." *Review* (Federal Reserve Bank of St. Louis), March 1977, pp. 2-17.

Cagan, Phillip. "The Effect of World Prices on U.S. Inflation." New York: NBER, 1977. Multilith.

Cagan, Phillip. *The Hydra Headed Monster. The Problem of Inflation in the United States.* Washington: American Enterprise Institute, 1974.

Cagan, Phillip. "Controls and Monetary Policy 1969-73." In *A New Look at Inflation.* Washington: American Enterprise Institute, 1973, pp. 1-34.

Cargill, T., and R. Meyer. "Some Time and Frequency Domain Distributed Lag Estimators: A Comparative Monte Carlo Study." *Econometrica* 42, no. 6 (November 1974): 1031-44.

Chou, Gregory. "Tests of Equality between Sets of Coefficients in Two Linear Regressions." *Econometrica* 27 (July 1960): 591-605.

Christ, Carl F. "Judging the Performance of Econometric Models of the U.S. Economy." *International Economic Review* 16, no. 1 (February 1975): 54-74.

Davis, Richard. "Implementing Open Market Policy with Monetary Aggregate Objectives." *Monetary Aggregates and Monetary Policy* (Federal Reserve Bank of New York), 1974, pp. 7-19.

Dutton, Dean. "Economics of Inflation and Output Fluctuations in the United States, 1952-74," *Journal of Monetary Economics* (1978), forthcoming.

Feige, Edgar, and Douglas Pearce. "The Substitutability of Money and Near-Monies: A Survey of the Time-Series Evidence." *Journal of Economic Literature* 15, no. 2 (June 1977): 439-69.

Fieleke, Norman S. "The Worldwide Inflation." *New England Economic Review* (Federal Reserve Bank of Boston), May/June 1976.

Friedman, Milton. *The Counter Revolution in Monetary Theory.* London: Institute of Economic Affairs for Wincott Foundation, 1970. Occasional Paper No. 33, p. 24.

Friedman, Milton. *The Optimum Quantity of Money and Other Essays.* Chicago: Aldine Pub. Co., 1969.

Friedman, Milton. "The Role of Monetary Policy." *American Economic Review* 58, no. 1 (March 1969): 1-17. Reprinted in M. Friedman. *The Optimum Quantity of Money and Other Essays*. University of Chicago, 1969, pp. 95-110.

Friedman, Milton. "The Quantity Theory of Money: A Restatement. "In Milton Friedman (ed.). *Studies in the Quantity Theory of Money.* University of Chicago, 1956.

Friedman, Milton, and Anna Schwartz. *A Monetary History of the United States*. Princeton University for NBER, 1963.

Frisch, Helmut. "Inflation Theory 1963-1975: A Second Generation 'Survey'." *Journal of Economic Literature* 15, no. 4 (December 1977).

Fromm, Gary, and Lawrence Klein. "A Comparison of Eleven Econometric Models of the United States." *American Economic Review* (May 1973): 385-93.

Goldfeld, Stephan. "The Case of the Missing Money." *BPEA* 3(1976): 638-730.

Goldfeld, Stephan. "The Demand for Money Revisited." *BPEA* 3(1973): 612-63.

Gordon, Robert J. "Can Inflation of the 1970's Be Explained?" *BPEA* 1(1977): 253-76.

Gordon, Robert J. "Recent Developments in the Theory of Inflation and Unemployment." *Journal of Monetary Economics* 2, no. 2 (April 1976): 185-220.

Gordon, Robert J. "The Impact of Aggregate Demand on Prices." *BPEA* 3(1975): 613-62.

Gordon, Robert J. "The Response of Wages and Prices to the First Two Years of Controls." *BPEA* 2(1973): 765-78.

Gordon, Robert J. "Wage/Price Controls and the Shifting Phillips Curve." *BPEA* 2(1972): 385-421.

Goreau, Louis M. "The Use of Compensatory Financing." *Finance and Development* 14, no. 3 (September 1977): 20-24.

Granger, C.W.J. "Investigating Causal Relations by Econometric Models and Cross Spectral Models." *Econometrica* 37 (July 1969): 424-38.

Hamburgher, Michael. "Behavior of the Money Stock: Is There a Puzzle?" *Journal of Monetary Economics* (July 1977).

Hamburgher, Michael J. "The Lag Effect of Monetary Policy: A Survey of Recent Literature." In *Monetary Aggregates and Monetary Policy* (Federal Reserve Bank of New York), 1974, pp. 104-13.

Hathaway, D. "Food Prices and Inflation." *BPEA* 1(1974): 63-109.

Haugh, L.D. "Checking the Independence of Two Covariance Stationary Time Series: A Univariate Residual Cross-Correlation Approach." *Journal of the American Statistical Association* (June 1976): 378-85.

Johnson, Harry. *On Economics and Society*. University of Chicago, 1975.

Johnson, Harry. "The Keynesian Revolution and the Monetarist Counter-revolution." *American Economic Review* 61, no. 2 (May 1971): 1-14. Reprinted in H. Johnson. *On Economics and Society*. University of Chicago, 1975, pp. 91-106.

Johnson, Jack. *Econometric Methods*. New York: McGraw-Hill, 1963.

Jessup, P., and M. Bochnak. "Money Market Mutual Funds: Their Impact on Banks." *Bank Administration* (September 1977): 28-32.

Kaldor, N. "Inflation and Recession in the World Economy." *The Economic Journal* 86 (December 1976): 703-14.

Karnosky, Denis. "The Link between Money and Prices, 1971-76."*Review* (Federal Reserve Bank of St. Louis), June 1976, pp. 17-23.

Keran, Michael. "Toward an Explanation of Simultaneous Inflation-Recession." *Business Review* (Federal Reserve Bank of San Francisco), Spring 1975, pp. 18-30.

Keran, Michael, and Michael Riordin. "Stabilization Policy in a World Context." *Economic Review* (Federal Reserve Bank of San Francisco), Fall 1976, pp. 5-19.

Levy, Michael. "Constraining Inflation: Causes, Complacencies and Evidence." *The Conference Board Record* 12, no. 10 (October 1975): 8-14.

Kosters, Marvin. *Controls and Inflation*. Washington: American Enterprise Institute, 1975.

Laidler, D.E.W., and J.M. Parkin. "Inflation—A Survey." *The Economic Journal*, no. 340 (December 1975): 741-809.

Lucas, R.E., Jr. "Expectations and the Neutrality of Money." *Journal of Economic Theory* 4, no. 2 (April 1972): 103-24.

Mayer, Thomas. "The Structure of Monetarism (I) and (II)." *Kredit and Kapital* (April and July 1975): 190-218 and 293-316. Reprinted in T. Mayer (ed.), *The Structure of Monetarism*. New York: W.W. Norton, 1978.

Meiselman, David I., and Arthur B. Laffer (eds.). *The Phenomenon of Worldwide Inflation*. Washington: American Enterprise Institute, 1975.

Mitchell, Daniel B. "Phase II Wage Controls." *Industrial and Labor Relations Review,* 27 (April 1974): 371-75.

Nobay, A. Robert, and H. Johnson. "Monetarism: A Historic-Theoretic Perspective." *Journal of Economic Literature* 15, no. 2 (June 1977): 470-85.

Nordhaus, William. "The Worldwide Wage Explosion." *BPEA* 2(1972): 431-64.

Niehans, Jürg. "How to Fill an Empty Shell." *American Economic Review* (May 1976): 177-83.

Manchester Conference Papers on Inflation in the World Economy. Published in M. Parkin and G. Zis (eds.). *Inflation in the World Economy.* University of Toronto Press, 1974.

Pierce, James, and Jared Enzler. "The Effects of External Inflationary Shocks." *BPEA* 1(1974): 13-54.

Poole, William. "Interpreting the Fed's Monetary Targets." *BPEA* 1(1976).

Pryor, Fred. "The Origins of Money." *Journal of Money, Credit and Banking* (August 1977): 391-409.

Sargent, Thomas J., and Neil Wallace. "Rational Expectations and the Theory of Economic Policy." *Journal of Monetary Economics* 2, no. 2 (April 1976): 169-83.

Schnittker, J. "The 1972-73 Food Price Spiral." *BPEA* 2(1973): 498-506.

Schwartz, Anna. "Secular Price Change in Historical Perspective." *Journal of Money, Credit and Banking* 5, no. 1, Part II (February 1973): 243-69.

Selden, Richard. "Inflation: Are We Winning the Fight?" *The Morgan Guarantee Survey* (October 1977): 7-13.

Shiller, Robert. "A Distributed Lag Estimator Derived from Smoothness Priors." *Econometrica* 41, no. 4 (July 1973): 775-88.

Shiller, Robert J. "Alternative Prior Representations of Smoothness for Distributed Lag Estimation." NBER *Working Paper No. 89.* NBER Computer Research Center, Cambridge, Massachusetts.

Sims, Christopher. "Distributed Lags." in M. Intriligator (ed.). *Frontiers of Quantitative Economics*, vol. 2. North Holland, 1974.

Sims, Christopher. "Money, Income and Causality." *American Economic Review* 62, no. 4. (September 1972): 540-52.

Staff Report of the Subcommittee on Domestic Monetary Policy of the Committee on Banking, Currency and Housing, House of Representatives. *The Impact of the Federal Reserve System's Monetary Policies on the Nation's Economy.* 94th Cong. 2d Sess., December 1976. Prepared by Robert E. Weintraub.

Stein, Jerome. (ed.). *Monetarism*. North Holland, 1976.

Stein, Jerome. "The Monetarist Criticism of the New Economics." In J. Stein (ed.). *Monetarism.* North Holland, 1976, pp. 1-16.

Waelbroeck, J. (ed.). *The Models of Project Link*. North Holland, 1976.

Index

Index

Almon, Shirley, 6, 19, 28-29, 30, 40
Almon lag coefficients, distribution of, 46-47, 48, 49
Andersen, Leonall, 3, 6, 23

Berner, Richard, 11
Brunner, Karl, 3

Cagan, Phillip, 11
Cargill, T., 48
Causality: direction, 33-34; direction, testing, 59-63; Granger definition of, 6, 7-8, 18, 20, 33; issue of, 2; tests of M_2-M_1 specification, 84; tests of M_2 specification, 81; tests of total reserves, 89-90
Chou, Gregory, 33
Clark, Peter, 11
Commerce, Department of, 104
Commercial bank time/savings deposit specification, 82-84
Controls, wage/price, 102-103
CPI, 25

Distributed lag models, estimation of, 27-28; interpretation of, 32-33; problems in, 28-29; sensitivity tests used for, 29-30; structural change in, 30-32

Econometric discovery, 28
Elasticity, money-price, stability of, 20, 23
Enzler, Jared, 11, 102-103, 104
Estimation residuals, distribution of, 49-50

Federal Reserve System, 2, 113-114, 116, 127; adoption of "bills only" policy by, 27; and anti-inflation money growth policy, 119-121; control of money stock by, 24; government security portfolio of, 8, 25, 77, 79, 91; and implications of monetarist inflation thesis, 8-9; lowering of M_1 growth rates by, 12-14; -Treasury "accord" (1951), 19, 27
Forecasting performance, post-1975, 53-54
Foreign influence, net, 105-107; expanding M_1 model to capture, 107
Friedman, Milton, 1, 3
Frisch, Helmut, 3

GNP, 25, 113
Gordon, Robert J., 11, 104
Goreau, Louis, 106
GPDP (gross private domestic product), 25
Granger, C.W.J., definition of causality by, 6, 7-8, 18, 20, 33, 40

House Concurrent Resolution 121, 133

IMF, 106
Inflation: accounting for unexplained (1973-1975), 9-12; associated with M_1 growth trends, 115-117; forecasts, post-1978, 117-118; money growth policy, anti-, 118-121; predominance of monetary (1971-1975), 6-7, 34-36; suggested explanation for surge in (1973/4-1974), 108-109; variability of M_1 growth and stability of, 121-127

Karnosky, Denis, 3, 6, 23, 35

Lag specification, approximating correct, 41-42
Lowrey, Barbara, 11

M_1 model, forward simulation with (1971/3-1975): close examination of forecast errors in, 100-107; introduction to and summary of,

M_1 model, (cont.)

93-97; overview of forecast errors in, 97-99; testing of monetarist inflation thesis with forecast errors in, 99-100. *See also under* Monetarist inflation model

M_1 specification, 5-6; defined, 2, 23-24; disaggregating, 46; growth, variability of, and stability of inflation, 121-127; growth-reduction program, recommendation of, 12-14; model estimations, complete, 58. *See also* Monetarist inflation model

M_2 specification, 7; causality tests of, 81; defined, 24, 77; sensitivity analysis of, 79-81

M_2-M_1, 82; causality tests of, 84; sensitivity analysis of, 82-84

M_3 specification, 7; defined, 24, 77; sensitivity analysis of, 85-87

M_3-M_2, estimations of, 87-88

M_4 specification, 7; defined, 24

M_5 specification, 7; defined, 24

Mayer, Thomas, 3

Mean absolute error (MAE), 7, 44, 48, 98

Meltzer, Allan, 3

Meyer, R., 48

Monetarism, 2-3, 4

Monetarist inflation model: approximating correct lag specification, 41-42; closer look at 10-quarter-lag M_1 model, 46-50; general, 20-23; introduction to testing of, with M_1 specification, 39-41; post-1971 stability testing of 10-quarter-lag M_1 model, 50-54; and sample period selection, 26-27; sensitivity analysis of 10-quarter-lag M_1 model (1963-1971), 42-46; and specifying monetary aggregate, 23-25; specifying of, 20-27; and time specification, 25-26

Monetarist inflation thesis, 2-3; and accounting for unexplained inflation (1973-1975), 9-12; defined, 3-4; findings on, 5-8; implications of, 8-9; introduction and overview to procedure for testing, 17-20; modeling of, 4-5; policy recommendation from study of, 12-14. *See also* Causality; Distributed lag models, estimation of; Inflation

Money growth-inflation relationship, 1-2; defined, 3-4; and monetarism, 2-3; stability and power of, 5. *See also* Monetarist inflation thesis

NBER, 105

Niehans, Jürg, 8, 14, 78; and Federal Reserve's government securities portfolio, 8, 25, 77, 79, 91

OECD, 105

Oil price hike, 2, 10-12, 19, 34-35, 100, 102; discussion of, 103-105

OLS (ordinary least squares), 6, 19; reliability of, as distributed lag estimation procedure, 29, 47-48

OPEC, 2, 19, 100, 102

Percent, percentage point, use of terms, 26

Pierce, James, 11, 102-103, 104

Poole, William, 127

Prices, primary commodity, 2, 10-11, 19

Project Link studies, 11, 105

Quantity theory of price determination, 3, 4

Recession (1974-1975), 1

Reserve(s): aggregate specifications, 7-8, 24-25, 77, 88-91; base, 8, 24, 77, 90-91; nonborrowed, 7, 24, 77, 90; total, 7-8, 24, 77, 88-90

RMSE (root mean square error), 43-44, 48

St. Louis Federal Reserve monetarism, 3, 4

Sample test(s): lengthening, 43-44, 51; overlapping, 51-52
Schwartz, Anna, 3
Sensitivity testing procedures (analysis), 18-19, 29-30; backward lengthening sample, 54; disaggregation, 46; lengthening sample, 43-44, 51; of M_2 specification, 79-81; of M_3 specification, 85-87; overlapping sample, 51-52; sideways straddle, 44; straddle, 44; straddle, with semiannual data, 45; of 10-quarter lag M_1 model (1963-1971), 42-46; of total reserves, 88-89
Shiller, Robert, 6, 19, 29
Shiller lag coefficients, distribution of, 47, 48, 49
Sims, Christopher, procedure of, for testing Granger definition of causality, 6, 7-8, 18, 20, 33, 40
Specification analysis, defined, 29
Straddle test(s), 29, 30, 44; with semiannual data, 45; sideways, 44
Structural change: in estimating distributed lag models, 30-32; testing for pre-1963, 54-59
Structural shift: defined, 31; of early 1960s, examination of, 58-59

Thrift deposit specification, 87-88
Treasury-Federal Reserve "accord" (1951), 19, 27

Wage/price approach, to explaining inflation, 1
Weights, uniform, 48-49
WPI, 25

About the Author

Peter I. Berman has been a senior economist at The Conference Board for the past two years. A graduate of Cornell University and The Johns Hopkins University, Dr. Berman has taught at the City University of New York and at Adelphi University. His work on monetary economics has appeared in *The Journal of Bank Research, International Technical Review, Eastern Economic Journal, American Economist, Papers* of the New York State Economics Association, and the *Bankers Magazine*.